Sharing the Dragon's Teeth

Terrorist Groups and the Exchange of New Technologies

Kim Cragin, Peter Chalk, Sara A. Daly, Brian A. Jackson

Prepared for the Department of Homeland Security

RAND   Homeland Security

A RAND INFRASTRUCTURE, SAFETY, AND ENVIRONMENT PROGRAM

This research was sponsored by the United States Department of Homeland Security and was conducted under the auspices of the Homeland Security Program within RAND Infrastructure, Safety, and Environment.

Library of Congress Cataloging-in-Publication Data

Sharing the dragon's teeth : terrorist groups and the exchange of new technologies / R. Kim Cragin ... [et al.].
    p. cm.
    "MG-485."
    Includes bibliographical references.
    ISBN 0-8330-3915-6 (pbk. : alk. paper)
    1. Terrorism. 2. Terrorism—Technological innovations. I. Cragin, Kim. II. Rand Corporation.

HV6431.S46655 2007
363.325—dc22

                                                                2006012871

The RAND Corporation is a nonprofit research organization providing objective analysis and effective solutions that address the challenges facing the public and private sectors around the world. RAND's publications do not necessarily reflect the opinions of its research clients and sponsors.

RAND® is a registered trademark.

Published 2007 by the RAND Corporation
1776 Main Street, P.O. Box 2138, Santa Monica, CA 90407-2138
1200 South Hayes Street, Arlington, VA 22202-5050
4570 Fifth Avenue, Suite 600, Pittsburgh, PA 15213-2665
RAND URL: http://www.rand.org/
To order RAND documents or to obtain additional information, contact
Distribution Services: Telephone: (310) 451-7002;
Fax: (310) 451-6915; Email: order@rand.org

Preface

This monograph is one component of a series of studies examining the technology competition between security organizations and terrorist organizations, a critical battleground in the war against terrorism. This series focuses on understanding how terrorist groups make technology choices and respond to the technologies deployed against them. Specifically, this book examines interactions among terrorist groups with a view toward assessing the potential for the exchange of technologies and knowledge. It also addresses the question of how effective such interactions are in bolstering group capabilities and presents a framework for evaluating interactions among terrorist organizations. To conduct the study, the authors traveled to the Philippines, Singapore, Lebanon, Israel, and the United Kingdom. This analysis should be of interest to homeland security policymakers in that it contributes to improved threat assessment and suggests new strategies to disrupt technology exchanges among terrorist organizations. In addition, as this investigation relies, in part, on analyses of technology exchange in legitimate organizations, it offers a novel methodological approach to comparative studies of terrorist organizations. The U.S. Department of Homeland Security sponsored the research.

The RAND Homeland Security Program

This research was conducted under the auspices of the Homeland Security Program within RAND Infrastructure, Safety, and Environment (ISE). The mission of ISE is to improve the development, operation, use, and protection of society's essential physical assets and natural resources and to enhance the related social assets of safety and security of individuals in transit and in their workplaces and communities. Homeland Security Program research supports the Department of Homeland Security and other agencies charged with preventing and mitigating the effects of terrorist activity within U.S. borders. Projects address critical infrastructure protection, emergency management, terrorism risk management, border control, first responders and preparedness, domestic threat assessments, domestic intelligence, and workforce and training.

Questions or comments about this monograph should be sent to the project leader, Brian A. Jackson (Brian_Jackson@rand.org). Information about the Homeland Security Program is available online (http://www.rand.org/ise/security/). Inquiries about research projects should be sent to the following address:

Michael Wermuth, Director
Homeland Security Program, ISE
RAND Corporation
1200 South Hayes Street
Arlington, VA 22202-5050
703-413-1100, x5414
Michael_Wermuth@rand.org

Contents

Figures

Tables

Summary

Operation Enduring Freedom and the global war on terrorism forced many members of al Qaeda to disperse, as the U.S. government and its allies removed safe havens and arrested a number of key leaders.[1] As a result, the nature of the terrorist threat against the United States appears to have changed. For example, some like-minded terrorist groups that perhaps do not have the global reach of a pre-9/11 al Qaeda nevertheless have formed regional alliances. Similarly, other events have caused terrorist groups that are not linked ideologically to form mutually beneficial partnerships. These partnerships have provided otherwise less capable terrorist groups with the opportunity to improve their skills and their reach. In each circumstance, emerging alliances could increase the threat that terrorism will pose to the United States in the next 3–15 years. Understanding these interactions, therefore, is essential to ongoing and future efforts in the U.S. global war on terrorism.

Terrorist groups in three areas—Mindanao, the West Bank and Gaza Strip, and southwest Colombia—have exchanged technologies and knowledge in an effort to improve their operational capabilities. Studying these situations, therefore, can provide the Department of Homeland Security (DHS) with examples of why and how terrorists might share new technologies in the future, as well as the degree to which these exchanges might be successful. We chose these case studies because the terrorist groups active in these regions are highly capable.

---

[1] For example, Ramzi Binalshib and Abu Zubaydah in 2002, Khalid Sheikh Mohammad and Hambali in 2003, Ahmed Khalfan Ghailani in 2004, and Abu Faraj Farj al-Libbi in 2005.

Thus, the technologies and exchange processes are weighed toward *success* and should be of significant concern to the U.S. national security community.

This book examines a variety of different technologies and exchange processes, ranging from remote-detonation devices to converted field ordnance to *katyusha* rockets. In some instances, terrorists successfully obtained and deployed the technologies involved. Counterterrorism forces disrupted other technology exchanges.

- In Mindanao, Indonesian Jemaah Islamiyah (JI) trained and equipped Filippino militants. New technologies included remote-detonation technologies and improvised explosive devices (IEDs), as well as pressure-activated switches designed to detonate bombs, should security forces attempt to deactivate them. These exchanges improved the operational effectiveness and tempo of militant groups in the region from approximately 2003 to 2005.
- In the West Bank and Gaza Strip, Hizballah trained and equipped Palestinian militants. New technologies included IEDs and *katyusha* rockets, as well as suicide detonation devices. These exchanges provided militants with the ability to continue to escalate attacks against Israel from approximately 2000 to 2005.
- In southwest Colombia, the Provisional Irish Republican Army (PIRA) trained and equipped militants in the Revolutionary Armed Forces of Colombia (or FARC, for Fuerzas Armadas Revolucionarios de Colombia) in the former demilitarized zone. New technologies and knowledge included remote-detonation technologies and Mark 18 "barracks-buster" mortars, as well as guerrilla warfare tactics. These skills helped FARC improve its urban warfare capabilities in 2001.

In total, we examined 11 terrorist groups that operate in these three regions. Our research into each revealed vulnerabilities in technology exchanges between terrorist organizations, which led to eight overarching conclusions. These conclusions relate to (1) improving threat assessments, (2) disrupting innovation processes, and (3) affecting terrorist groups' cost-benefit analyses.

Improving Threat Assessments

Primarily, our research reemphasized the need for accurate, up-to-date threat assessments of terrorist groups. More importantly, our findings indicate that a threat assessment that ignores intergroup dynamics—including technology exchanges and beyond—is destined to be out-dated quickly. These assessments would also benefit, according to our research, from a close examination of failed attacks. If terrorist groups attempt a particular tactic over and over again, this might represent an area in which they would invest in a new technology.

Similarly, the terrorist groups in our study weighed potential gains or costs in *operational capabilities* as more important than ideological similarities when choosing whether or not to participate in technology exchanges. For example, JI transferred technologies to like-minded Filipino militants, but in exchange derived *operational benefits* from access to safe havens in Mindanao. Hizballah similarly transferred knowledge to Palestinian militants through direct person-to-person contact, but only until Israeli counterterrorism forces began to arrest Hizballah's skilled trainers. It then shifted toward a more remote transfer of descriptive information of physical technology without instruction. This finding suggests that threat assessments should focus on operational as well as strategic motivations for alliances between terrorist groups.

Finally, analyses of individuals with technical knowledge tend to focus on chemical, biological, radiological, or nuclear (CBRN) technologies. While we do not want to detract from the importance of monitoring individuals with these technical skills, our findings suggest that analysts also should monitor individuals with technical expertise in remote-detonation technologies, rockets and missiles, IEDs, and converted field ordnances (mortars).

Disrupting Innovation Processes

We also discovered some factors that facilitated the exchange of technology between terrorist groups. In addressing these facilitating factors, the U.S. government should disrupt innovation processes and reduce the potential for a successful exchange of technology. For example, in both Mindanao and southwest Colombia, terrorist groups transferred technologies most successfully through direct, person-to-person training. Terrorist groups could interact closely, because governments had provided them with *safe havens* as incentives for their participation in peace negotiations. Our findings question the utility of such an approach, especially if these safe havens are not monitored closely by third parties.

Additionally, the easy movement of people and goods across borders also facilitated the technology exchanges. In the cases of Hizballah and JI, these militant groups utilized existing smuggling routes to transport equipment and trainers. At least three PIRA members traveled from the United Kingdom to Colombia, without getting stopped by security officials. This suggests that tightening border security practices should also help disrupt technology exchanges between terrorist groups. In circumstances in which the U.S. government does not control borders yet is concerned about technology exchanges, it should consider providing appropriate training and equipment to these government authorities.

Finally, in the case of Hizballah and Palestinian militants, Israeli counterterrorism policies aimed at targeting individuals with technical skills served to disrupt advances in the groups' capabilities. In Chapter Six, we suggest that the U.S. intelligence community monitor the movement of individuals with technical skills, such as deploying remote-detonation devices, as well as CBRN weapon technology. We would also suggest that the U.S. government consider arresting these terrorists, should it become apparent that they are sharing knowledge across militant groups of concern to the United States. The U.S. government has already adopted this approach in certain areas, for example in Southeast Asia with its rewards program for JI militants in the Philippines. But, for the most part, U.S. programs focus on militants with links to al Qaeda. Our research suggests that these types of programs be expanded to include individuals with certain technical skills, in addition to leaders who have links to al Qaeda.

Affecting Terrorist Groups' Cost-Benefit Analyses

Our research indicates that the U.S. government would benefit from policies aimed at undermining the trust between terrorist organizations. In all three of our case studies, terrorists built on a foundation of trust when deciding to interact closely, as well as when these groups actually exchanged the technologies. To fracture this trust, U.S. policymakers could reveal suspicious leaks in groups' information security. Or, for cases in which money transfers occur, disrupt payment. These policies could help to exacerbate natural religious, political, or ethnic cleavages between these groups and create suspicion that individuals of the other group might turn trainers in to local authorities. With regard to other influence campaigns, U.S. security authorities might develop programs that attempt to change perceptions of a common enemy. Such policies would likely increase the costs associated with technology exchanges, reducing their potential for success.

Conclusion

DHS, in cooperation with other government agencies, is responsible for protecting the U.S. homeland against terrorist attacks. One way in which DHS can fulfill this responsibility is by anticipating and preparing for terrorist group innovations. Clearly, most innovations will take place beyond U.S. borders, but lessons learned could be applied to attacks inside the United States. Monitoring this flow of information and learning, therefore, is a key homeland security task. By examining how terrorist groups exchange technology and knowledge, this study provides DHS and other national security policymakers with some insight into the innovation process. It also suggests ways in which government policies can erect barriers to terrorists' adoption of new technologies.

Acknowledgments

The authors would like to thank Michael Wermuth, Juliette Kayyem, and David Mosher for their thoughtful comments on earlier drafts of this monograph. Special thanks also to those individuals in Southeast Asia, the United Kingdom, Lebanon, and Israel who aided us in our research for this study. We have not mentioned their names at their request. Any mistakes, of course, are the sole responsibility of the authors.

Abbreviations

ARMM	Autonomous Region of Muslim Mindanao
ASG	Abu Sayyaf Group
CBRN	chemical, biological, radiological, nuclear
CIRA	Continuity Irish Republican Army
DHS	U.S. Department of Homeland Security
ETA	Basque Fatherland and Liberty (Euskadi Ta Askatasuna)
FARC	Revolutionary Armed Forces of Colombia (Fuerzas Armadas Revolucionarios de Colombia)
Hamas	Islamic Resistance Movement (Harakat al-Muqawama al-Islamiya)
IDF	Israel Defense Forces
IED	improvised explosive device
JI	Jemaah Islamiyah
MBG	Misuari Breakaway Group
MILF	Moro Islamic Liberation Front
MNLF	Moro National Liberation Front
PA	Palestinian Authority

PIJ	Palestinian Islamic Jihad
PIRA	Provisional Irish Republican Army
PLO	Palestinian Liberation Organization
RIRA	Real Irish Republican Army
RSRM	Rajah Soliaman Revolutionary Movement
RUC	Royal Ulster Constabulary
SPCPD	Southern Philippine Council for Peace and Development
WBGS	West Bank and Gaza Strip
UAV	unmanned aerial vehicle

CHAPTER ONE

Introduction

> Cadmus made a furrow in the ground, and planted the dragon's teeth. . . . Scarce had he done so when the clods began to move, and the points of spears to appear above the surface. Next helmets with their nodding plumes came up, and next the shoulders and breasts and limbs of men with weapons, and in time a harvest of armed warriors.[1]

Terrorists, more often than not, challenge state adversaries that have more resources at their disposal, including soldiers with better training and equipment. Unlike the characters in the above quote from Greek mythology, however, terrorists do not have access to dragon's teeth that they can plant to "grow" new fighters and weapons. Thus, terrorists attempt to overcome this asymmetry by seizing the initiative from states. They attack unprotected or vulnerable targets at seemingly random intervals. Terrorists also overcome this asymmetry through innovation: Al Qaeda members used box knives to hijack planes and turn them into explosive devices as they attacked the World Trade Center in New York City and the Pentagon near Washington, D.C. Preventing terrorists from seizing the initiative and innovating new technologies and tactics is, therefore, a key aspect of U.S. homeland security.

This book examines how terrorist groups exchange technologies and knowledge, suggesting ways in which the United States could dis-

---

[1] Adapted from Thomas Bulfinch, *Mythology: The Age of Fable, the Age of Chivalry, Legends of Charlemagne*, New York: Crowell, 1970.

rupt this process and thereby protect the U.S. homeland. To do this, we ask four fundamental questions:

1. How have terrorist groups attempted to exchange technologies and knowledge?
2. What effects did these exchanges have on the capabilities of relevant terrorist groups?
3. What can we learn about the vulnerabilities of terrorist groups, given the exchange process?
4. How can the U.S. government best exploit these vulnerabilities?

Some might argue that policymakers both within and outside the United States always have been concerned about interactions between terrorist groups. For example, governments in the 1970s and 1980s were alarmed at the relationships between the Provisional Irish Republican Army (PIRA), Basque Fatherland and Liberty (ETA, for Euskadi Ta Askatasuna), and the Palestinian Liberation Organization (PLO). This concern, moreover, was evident particularly when it came to terrorists sharing new technologies or information about their use. We agree. Yet we suggest that the potential for terrorists to share among themselves is an even greater threat in a post-9/11 world. The United States is the sole remaining superpower and is therefore a global target. Ideological barriers and issues of distrust are less likely to exist within the umbrella of the wider al Qaeda organization. Similarly, the global nature of this group makes it more likely to risk helping others.

Understanding Terrorist Threats

Combating terrorism begins with an understanding of the threats that myriad militant groups pose to the United States. Achieving this understanding is a complex challenge. For example, it is difficult to compare terrorist groups with each other: One group might have better reach into the United States, while another uses more sophisticated technology. In general, terrorist groups are assessed according to a combination of motivations (e.g., do they articulate hatred toward the United States?) as well as capabilities (e.g., do they have the capability to attack the United States?). Some militant groups might truly hate the United States but be unable to conduct a successful attack. Other highly capable groups could simply be uninterested in attacking U.S. targets, although they could do so successfully if they desired. Figure 1.1 was developed in 2002 by analysts in RAND Project AIR FORCE.[2] It presents one concept of how the threats that a variety of terrorist groups might pose to the United States can be compared with each other.

In this book, we focus exclusively on how terrorist groups might improve their capabilities through an exchange of technologies. That is, our research is concerned with movement along the x-axis (capabilities) in Figure 1.1. We do not address concerns of whether or not any given terrorist group *might want* to attack the United States (y-axis). Having said that, all three of the militant groups in the upper right quadrant—those that evidence high capability and hostile intentions against the United States—are incorporated into this book. Our research also excludes any capability enhancements that terrorist groups might undertake on their own, focusing instead on *interactions* between terrorist groups.

Having defined the parameters of this study, we would argue that terrorist interactions are a key aspect of understanding terrorist threats. These interactions allow terrorist groups to elevate the threat that they pose to state governments by sharing "best practices" and therefore multiplying their own efforts with the knowledge and know-how from other militant groups. This potential threat is particularly true with regard to al Qaeda. Since Operation Enduring Freedom in Afghanistan and the advent of the global war on terrorism, the U.S. government has engaged in a series of activities aimed at dismantling al Qaeda. These activities range from destroying financial networks to targeting key al Qaeda leaders to changing regimes in Afghanistan. As a result, al

---

[2]   For more information, see Kim Cragin and Sara A. Daly, *The Dynamic Terrorist Threat: An Assessment of Group Motivations and Capabilities in a Changing World*, Santa Monica, Calif.: RAND Corporation, MR-1782-AF, 2004.

Figure 1.1
Assessing Terrorist Threats Against the United States

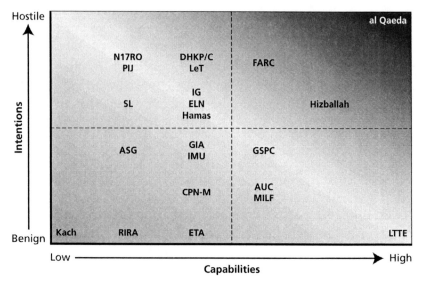

NOTE: N17RO = Revolutionary Organization November 17. DHKP/C = Revolutionary People's Liberation Party/Front. FARC = Revolutionary Armed Forces of Colombia. PIJ = Palestinian Islamic Jihad. LeT = Lashkar e-Toiba. IG = Al Gama'at al-Islamiyya. SL = Shining Path. ELN = National Liberation Army. GIA = Armed Islamic Group. GSPC = Salafist Group for Preaching and Combat. IMU = Islamic Movement of Uzbekistan. AUC = Self-Defense Forces of Colombia. CPN-M = Communist Party of Nepal–Maoist. MILF = Moro Islamic Liberation Front. RIRA = Real Irish Republican Army. ETA = Basque Fatherland and Liberty. LTTE = Liberation Tigers of Tamil Eelam. For more information about these groups, see the appendix.
RAND *MG485-1.1*

Qaeda the organization has become less and less structured, comprised of loose networks of like-minded organizations that sometimes cooperate and other times do not. According to Fawaz Gerges, many of the militant groups associated with al Qaeda have struggled with whether or not they should focus on "near enemies," such as the Egyptian or Pakistani governments, or "far enemies," such as the United States.[3] Understanding the implications of cooperation between these groups in the future—including what might motivate such cooperation and

---

[3] Fawaz A. Gerges, *The Far Enemy: Why Jihad Went Global*, Cambridge and New York: Cambridge University Press, 2005.

how it might improve militant groups' capabilities—can help analysts and policymakers better gauge threats to the United States.

Methodology and Parameters

This book begins with the premise that terrorist groups are, in fact, organizations. Terrorist groups share characteristics with other, non-violent organizations, including businesses, nonprofit institutions, and even the government. As such, a primary goal of terrorist organizations is self-perpetuation. We, therefore, draw on organizational theory to establish our research parameters and as a framework to interpret our empirical findings. As such, key research themes in organizational theory include groups' rationale or motivations to exchange technologies, the characteristics of these technologies, and the processes by which organizations exchange technologies and knowledge, as well as the outcomes.

We use the terms *technology exchange* and *knowledge exchange* throughout this book. By *technology exchange*, we attempt to capture the means by which terrorists share physical tools and devices. So, for example, a technology exchange might include one terrorist group smuggling communications equipment into a conflict area to be adopted by another. By *knowledge exchange*, we attempt to capture tactical plans, intelligence, and other information including the data and expertise needed to use specific technologies well. For example, a knowledge exchange might include one terrorist group teaching another how to deploy an antitank missile or camouflage an IED. Having said that, in some circumstances, technology and knowledge are *transferred* from one group to another, in contrast to a mutually beneficial exchange. A thorough examination of environments in which technology might be exchanged successfully with an alternative technology or knowledge versus environments in which technology and knowledge are transferred is beyond the scope of this book. Instead, we focus primarily on the rationale for and processes of the exchange or transfer of technology and knowledge.

Given our understanding of organizational theory, we would expect that the effects of technology and knowledge exchanges on terrorist group capabilities would vary considerably. New technology or knowledge could

- increase operational range—enable the group to do new things that it could not do before. New options may enable entirely new activities (e.g., new weapons or training that open a new attack mode) or may provide more options for carrying out the same operation.
- increase operational effectiveness—improve the group's ability to do things that it could already do, but do them better (e.g., with increasing lethality, reduced risk, or higher probability of success)
- increase operational efficiency—allow the group to carry out activities that it already can carry out, but do so at less cost in time, resources, or other inputs.

We then explore three empirical case studies of exchanges between terrorist groups. Our case studies include exchanges between Jemaah Islamiyah (JI) and other Islamist[4] militant groups in Mindanao, transfers from Hizballah to Palestinian militants in the West Bank and Gaza Strip, and exchanges between PIRA and the Revolutionary Armed Forces of Colombia (FARC, for Fuerzas Armadas Revolucionarios de Colombia) in southwest Colombia. We chose these case studies for a number of reasons. Primarily, JI, Hizballah, and FARC are all highly capable militant organizations. Figure 1.1, for example, identifies both Hizballah and FARC as highly capable and highly motivated to attack the United States. Because al Qaeda—the third group in the upper right corner of Figure 1.1—has become fractured as part of the global war on terrorism, we decided to use JI as a representative for al Qaeda in this study. JI has a similar ideological foundation to al Qaeda

---

[4] We use this term to delineate and designate militants who adhere to the Salafi Jihad Movement. That is, they believe that Muslims worldwide should be ruled by religious leaders, rather than secular leaders. They also believe that violence is the primary means to achieve this goal.

and many experts view it as a smaller, "regional" al Qaeda in Southeast Asia (see Chapter Three). We believed that by examining highly capable terrorist groups, our case studies would be biased toward the *most successful*—and therefore potentially the most worrisome—technology exchanges. Additionally, any problems that highly capable groups experience in exchanging technologies should be significant barriers to others, since these groups are the most likely to be successful.

We also chose these three cases because, with the exception of PIRA, the terrorist groups involved maintain a high operational tempo. We therefore believed that the case studies would be the *most expansive*, with regard to the types of technologies exchanged. We also hoped that we would be able to identify shifts in technology usage more readily, simply because more examples would exist.

Finally, we anticipated that the rationale and motivations for exchange would differ widely across our three case studies. For example, JI shares an ideological worldview and overarching objective with other Islamist militant groups in Southeast Asia. We therefore expected that JI's rationale for engaging in technology exchanges would be ideologically driven. Hizballah and most Palestinian militants, however, derive from different, albeit Islamic, ideologies. With regard to Hizballah's rationale, we therefore estimated that it would be driven more by its enmity toward Israel than by religious ideology. Finally, we expected that PIRA and FARC would represent the most disparate ideological worldviews, exchanging technologies exclusively for profit. Given these different rationales, any underlying similarities in exchanges between these militant groups, revealed by our research, should be significant findings.

Subsequent chapters examine all the terrorist groups relevant to our case studies in greater detail, but we provide a brief description of each below as a reference.

- **Abu Sayyaf Group (ASG).** This militant group operates primarily in Mindanao, southern Philippines. It rejects the 1995 Davao Consensus, establishing the Autonomous Region of Muslim Mindanao, and wants to establish an independent Islamic state in Mindanao. The ASG is generally considered to have approximately 100–200 members.

- **Al-Aqsa Martyrs Brigades.** This militant group operates in the West Bank and Gaza Strip. It formed following the advent of the al-Aqsa Intifada in October 2000 and is a faction of the nationalist Palestinian Fatah movement. Membership is unknown.

- **The Islamic Resistance Movement, better known as Hamas (for Harakat al-Muqawama al-Islamiya).** This militant group operates in the West Bank and Gaza Strip. It fights for an Islamic Palestinian state. Members have conducted a number of suicide bombings against civilians in Israel. Israeli security forces assassinated Hamas founder and former leader Yasin in April 2004. The militant wing of Hamas has been estimated at approximately 150 members, with a total membership of approximately 5,000.

- **Hizballah.** This militant group operates primarily in southern Lebanon. Its ideology is Shia and it has close ties with Iran. From 1983 to 2000, Hizballah members fought against the Israeli military presence in Lebanon. Since the Israeli military withdrawal, Hizballah members have run for the Lebanese parliament. The U.S. State Department notes that Hizballah has several thousand supporters and a few hundred militants.[5]

- **Jemaah Islamiyah (JI).** This militant group operates primarily in Indonesia, although it allegedly has a presence in southern Thailand, Malaysia, Singapore, and the Philippines. Its rhetorical goal is to establish a pan-regional Islamic Caliphate in Southeast Asia. JI members were responsible for the October 2002 attack on a nightclub in Bali. Estimates of JI membership range from several hundred to thousands.

- **Moro Islamic Liberation Front (MILF).** This militant group operates primarily in Mindanao, southern Philippines. Its members have rejected the 1995 Davao Consensus and want an independent Islamic state in the area. It has approximately 12,000 members.

---

[5] U.S. Department of State, *Country Reports on Terrorism*, Washington, D.C.: U.S. Department of State, Office of the Coordinator for Counterterrorism, April 27, 2005.

- **Misuari Breakaway Group–Moro National Liberation Front (MBG-MNLF).** This militant group operates primarily in Mindanao. Its members are former fighters from the MNLF, which negotiated the aforementioned Davao Consensus. It is widely believed to operate in conjunction with ASG. Membership is unknown.
- **Palestinian Islamic Jihad (PIJ).** This militant group operates in the West Bank and Gaza Strip. It fights for the formation of an independent Islamic Palestinian state. Smaller than Hamas, it only has approximately 100 members. Its founder and leader, Fathi al-Shikaki, was assassinated by Israeli security forces in 1995.
- **Provisional Irish Republican Army (PIRA).** This militant group, commonly referred to as the *IRA*, fought against British rule in Northern Ireland. Its political wing, Sinn Fein, negotiated with the UK government as part of the 1998 Good Friday Accords. PIRA has officially disbanded.
- **Rajah Soliaman Revolutionary Movement (RSRM).** This militant group operates primarily in Mindanao. The group reportedly was started in 2002 to establish a theocratic Islamic state in the Philippines. It allegedly has a special task force for urban attacks. Membership is unknown.
- **Revolutionary Armed Forces of Colombia (FARC, for Fuerzas Armadas Revolucionarios de Colombia).** This militant group operates primarily in rural Colombia. The group wants a Marxist revolution in the country. It has approximately 12,000 members.

Monograph Structure

Chapter Two outlines key concepts in organizational theory that we believe are the most relevant to our understanding of exchanges between terrorist groups. Chapter Three explores how technology and knowledge exchanges occur between militant groups in Southeast Asia. In particular, we focus on explosive weapon technology in Mindanao, southern Philippines. Chapter Four examines how Lebanese Hizballah has attempted to provide technology and knowledge to Palestinian militants in an effort to aid their fight against Israel. Chapter Five assesses the 2001 arrest of three PIRA militants in southwest Colombia and the exchange of technology and knowledge, especially as it relates to urban warfare, between PIRA and FARC. Finally, Chapter Six addresses the policy implications of our findings and suggests ways to disrupt the successful exchange of technology and knowledge among terrorist groups.

CHAPTER TWO

Organizational Theory and Terrorism

Militant groups threaten their adversaries in part through the combination of technology and knowledge. By sharing best practices or learning from each other's mistakes, militant groups can improve their operational capability. These exchanges, therefore, are a key national security issue for the U.S. government in general and the Department of Homeland Security (DHS) specifically. This chapter provides an overarching picture of how organizations adopt new technologies in general, so that we can better understand, and account for, exchanges between terrorist groups. To do this, we explore the academic literature on organizational theory, focusing on how technology and knowledge is exchanged between organizations in general to gain a greater understanding of terrorist groups.

Pursuing New Technologies

Organizational theory holds two analytical frameworks that are relevant to our study of how terrorist groups share best practices. The first, *technology diffusion*, emphasizes the passive spread of specific technologies from group to group. The second, *technology adoption*, emphasizes the more active decision taken by groups to exchange or receive a new technology. We discuss these approaches in greater detail below.

Technology Diffusion

Technology diffusion draws on models of the spread of disease in susceptible populations. In this context, experts view the diffusion of technologies as the epidemic spread of information from individuals or organizations that know about a new technology to those that do not. The analytical approach to determine the process of technology diffusion requires that researchers begin with the outcome—e.g., the spread of technology among groups—and work backward in an attempt to capture why some organizations did and did not absorb the new technology. Figure 2.1 illustrates this approach. Each spot within the diagram illustrates a different organization. The analyst would therefore begin with the population or collection of spots furthest to the right, identifying the spread of darkened (e.g., "infected") spots, and work backward to the population furthest to the left to identify the source and patterns of exchange.

The underlying assumption of technology diffusion theory is that potential users of a new technology will absorb it when and if they learn of its existence, as long as barriers to that uptake do not exist. Similarly, it assumes that information about technology is spread through contact between potential new and current users.[1] But this approach has serious limitations. Primarily, it treats some potential new users of technology as passive recipients of information, thereby omitting the

Figure 2.1
The Diffusion of Technology over Time

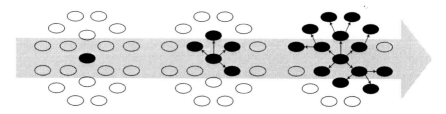

---

[1]   So, for example, Holden's analysis of the "contagiousness" of airline hijackings specifically draws on this sort of "disease" transmission framework to explain the spread of a specific tactic. See Robert T. Holden, "The Contagiousness of Aircraft Hijacking," *The American Journal of Sociology*, Vol. 91, No. 4, January 1986, pp. 874–904. See also A. Griliches, "Hybrid Corn: An Exploration in the Economics of Technological Change," *Econometrica*, Vol. 48, 1957, pp. 501–522; and E. Mansfield, "Technical Change and the Rate of Imitation," *Econometrica*, Vol. 29, No. 4, 1961, pp. 741–766.

factors that influence whether those organizations are even interested in attempting technology exchange activities.

Technology Adoption

To address this passivity problem, technology adoption studies focus on specific elements that affect the spread of a technology from one organization to another. When faced with a new challenge, organizations must make a decision about the appropriate response to that problem. Technology exchange is one of many possible solutions. The theory, therefore, posits that a group will only pursue a new technology if it is convinced—an active decision—that the technology will solve the group's current problem.[2]

Importantly, the theory stipulates that organizations make the decision to pursue new technologies under conditions of uncertainty. This uncertainty leads to two primary risks: (1) the risk that the group's cost-benefit judgments about the technology are incorrect and, as a result, its decision may be wrong, and (2) the risk that its attempt to adopt the technology will fail and it will pay the costs of adopting without gaining the compensating benefits. An organization is likely to attempt to reduce these risks by seeking out more information and expertise before committing itself. Gathering such information takes time and effort, however. A group's judgment whether to pursue a technology exchange activity at a given time will therefore be based on what net benefit is required, how certain it must be of that benefit, and how much risk of failure it is willing to take in the adoption effort.[3]

Experts have identified a range of factors that can shape an organization's judgment about the costs and benefits of a technology and its ability to gather information to reduce the risks associated with new activities.[4] We have listed these factors in Table 2.1. Notably, in most

---

2 Peter J. Lane and Michael Lubatkin, "Relative Absorptive Capacity and Interorganizational Learning," *Strategic Management Journal*, Vol. 19, No. 5, 1998, pp. 461–477.

3 Everett M. Rogers, *Diffusion of Innovations*, New York: The Free Press, 1995.

4 See Rui Baptista, "The Diffusion of Process Innovations: A Selective Review," *International Journal of the Economics of Business*, Vol. 6, No. 1, 1999, pp. 107–129; and Rogers (1995) for further discussion.

cases, the theory indicates that organizations choose between adopting and *deferring* the acquisition of a new technology, rather than between adopting and *rejecting* it.[5]

Although these factors provide a fuller understanding of an organization's decision to adopt a new technology, they do not consider factors that influence whether a receiving organization can take up the technology successfully.[6] The issue of knowledge is particularly important for understanding when and how technology exchange interactions between different organizations will succeed or fail. Indeed, research has shown that the "mere existence" of interactions among organizations is not enough for success.[7]

Absorbing New Technologies Successfully

For any given new technology to be effective, the receiving organization also must have the appropriate knowledge to use the technology successfully. A number of different factors affect how an organization might utilize a new technology and whether this utilization is effective: (1) characteristics of the technology itself, (2) characteristics of the receiving and source organizations, and (3) characteristics of the actual exchange mode. The following sections explore these factors more thoroughly.

Characteristics of the Technology

Certain types of technology are straightforward. *Explicit knowledge*—information embedded in physical technologies (e.g., assault rifles) or captured in written instructions—can be exchanged through little more than handing it from one person to another, provided they share

---

[5]   Whether or not a group will "change its mind" later will be affected by the openness of the group and its decisionmakers to new information and a willingness to revisit their initial judgments.

[6]   See, for example, discussion in Baptista (1999).

[7]   Lane and Lubatkin (1998).

Table 2.1
Factors Affecting Technology Adoption Decisions

Category	Attribute	Description
Technology	Comparative advantage	Technologies with larger apparent advantages compared with currently available options will be more readily adopted.
	Compatibility	Technologies that appear compatible with the current ways the organization operates will be easier to adopt.
	Complexity	How simple or complex a technology appears affects perceptions of how risky it will be to adopt.
	Trialability or observability	"Test driving" a technology before committing to adopt can provide significant information and reduce adoption risks. Although inferior to trying the technology itself, directly observing its use can provide information to reduce adoption risk.
	Price	The more expensive a technology is to a group, the higher the stakes in deciding to adopt it.
The group and its social systems	Internal group decision structures	Depending on the authority and other structures within the group, adoption decisions could be made collectively or individually. The nature of these internal structures could affect when and how a group decides to pursue a new technology.
	Communication channels	A group's ability to gather additional information to inform its adoption decision and reduce the inherent risks involved depends on the nature of the communication channels available to it.
	External environment	Activities by organizations or individuals outside the group can affect the adoption decision. For example, external proponents of change seeking to "sell" a group on a specific technology could contribute to its adoption decision. More generally, the spread of a technology among other groups could provide a less focused, but still relevant, pressure on a group to adopt it.

SOURCES: Adapted from Baptista (1999) and Rogers (1995).

a common language that can be used in the transmission.[8] Subsequent studies of technology exchanges, however, have shown that sharing explicit knowledge was frequently not enough to allow the receiving organization to duplicate the capabilities of the source organization. Thus, experts delineated another class of knowledge: *tacit knowledge.* Tacit knowledge is less well-defined knowledge, for example, individuals' "know-how" that they build through experience or "the accumulated practical skills that allow one to do something smoothly and efficiently."[9] Notably, organizations often must use both explicit and tacit knowledge to adopt a new technology successfully and address its operational challenges.

Beyond the overarching distinction between explicit and tacit knowledge, a variety of related characteristics also can affect the relative ease or difficulty of exchanging specific technologies from one organization to another. Table 2.2 summarizes these characteristics.

Characteristics of the Receiving Organization

An organization's *absorptive capacity* derives from the knowledge and capability that the organization already possesses when it seeks to absorb new knowledge. A group needs a sufficient base of knowledge related to the new technology so that it can understand the technology and put it to use.[10] For example, an organization seeking to acquire biological weapon technologies that had previous experience only with conventional weapons likely would have difficulty absorbing this technology from another group without a significant input of new knowledge.

---

[8]   Robert M. Grant, "Toward a Knowledge-Based Theory of the Firm," *Strategic Management Journal,* Vol. 17, 1996, pp. 109–122.

[9]   Bruce Kogut and Udo Zander, "Knowledge of the Firm, Combinative Capabilities, and the Replication of Technology," *Organization Science,* Vol. 3, No. 3, 1992, pp. 383–397.

[10]   Brian A. Jackson, John C. Baker, Peter Chalk, Kim Cragin, John V. Parachini, and Horacio R. Trujillo, *Aptitude for Destruction,* Vol. 1: *Organizational Learning in Terrorist Groups and Its Implications for Combating Terrorism,* Santa Monica, Calif.: RAND Corporation, MG-331-NIJ, 2005a.

Table 2.2
Technology Characteristics That Affect Exchange

Characteristic	Effect
Explicit vs. tacit	Explicit knowledge, because it is embodied in physical objects or codified, is more easily exchanged than tacit knowledge.
Teachable vs. nonteachable	Technologies that are easier to teach are more readily exchangeable.
Observable in use vs. nonobservable	Elements of a technology that can be directly observed—e.g., by an individual being trained in the use of a weapon—are more exchangeable than those that are not obvious to an observer.
Simple vs. complex	Because of their ease of communication, simple technologies are more readily exchangeable than more complex technologies.
Independent vs. system technologies	Technologies that can be used as stand-alone units, rather than those that depend on integration into larger systems, are easier to exchange.
General purpose vs. specialized	Technologies that can be used for many things and in many contexts are easier to exchange than those that are only applicable to specific tasks.
Easily aggregated vs. idiosyncratic	Knowledge that can be aggregated— e.g., numerical information that can be expressed in common formats, individual instructions that can be assembled into larger manuals—is easier to exchange than idiosyncratic knowledge that is specific to individual circumstances, times, or environments and difficult to express in aggregate forms.

SOURCES: Adapted from Jeffrey L. Cummings, *Knowledge Transfer Across R&D Units: An Empirical Investigation of the Factors Affecting Successful Knowledge Transfer Across Intra- and Inter-Organizational Units*, unpublished doctoral dissertation, Washington, D.C.: School of Business and Public Management, George Washington University, 2002; Gunnar Hedlund, "A Model of Knowledge Management and the N-Form Corporation," *Strategic Management Journal*, Vol. 15 (Special Issue), Strategy: Search for New Paradigms, 1994, pp. 73–90; Rogers (1995, p. 12); and Bernard Simonin, "Ambiguity and the Process of Knowledge Exchange in Strategic Alliances," *Strategic Management Journal*, Vol. 20, No. 7, 1999, pp. 598–623 [pp. 598–599].

Beyond the specific area of absorptive capacity, research also indicates that the receiving organization's more general learning capabilities may also affect its ability to benefit from knowledge exchanges from other organizations.[11] An organization could have developed these learning capabilities, for example, through its past experience with acquiring new technologies and innovations.[12] Alternatively, the organization simply could possess enough slack resources and time to assess and "metabolize" the new knowledge. Finally, an organization's absorptive capacity is likely to be high if its internal culture is generally open to new approaches and technologies.[13] Whether or not the organization has mechanisms in place to retain and institutionalize new knowledge in its operations will also affect the overall outcomes of exchange activities.[14]

Characteristics of the Source Organization

Characteristics of the source organization also affect the knowledge exchange's potential for success. Not unexpectedly, the source's strategic intent and motives (do they actually intend to help the receiver organization?[15]) and the level of trust between the two groups are important.[16] Beyond basic trust, past research also demonstrates that the level of social cohesion in the relationship between the two organizations—for example, direct interpersonal relationships—also can

---

[11] Jackson et al. (2005a); Brian A. Jackson, John C. Baker, Peter Chalk, Kim Cragin, John V. Parachini, and Horacio R. Trujillo, *Aptitude for Destruction*, Vol. 2: *Case Studies of Organizational Learning in Five Terrorist Groups*, Santa Monica, Calif.: RAND Corporation, MG-332-NIJ, 2005b.

[12] Rogers (1995).

[13] Cummings (2002).

[14] Gabriel Szulanski, "Exploring Internal Stickiness: Impediments to the Transfer of Best Practice Within the Firm," *Strategic Management Journal*, Vol. 17 (Winter Special Issue), 1996, pp. 27–43.

[15] Cummings (2002).

[16] Andrew C. Inkpen, "Learning, Knowledge Acquisition, and Strategic Alliances," *European Management Journal*, Vol. 16, No. 2, 1998, pp. 223–229.

affect the willingness of the source organization to commit itself to making the knowledge exchange successful.[17]

In examining the nature of the source organization in a knowledge exchange, the level of "match" between that group and the potential receiver organization is critical. Although there must be differences in the technical levels of the two organizations for there to be technologies worth exchanging between them, too much divergence could make the interaction more difficult.[18] Previous research also has shown that dissimilarities among organizations in their cultures, beliefs, and levels of education can limit the effectiveness of the exchange.[19] Having said that, initial differences among organizations can be overcome if the relationship between the two groups endures over a period of time.[20] Finally, research clearly demonstrates that, if the source organization has previously encountered and addressed problems similar to what the receiving organization is facing, the exchange is more likely to be effective.[21]

Characteristics of the Transmission Mode

For technology to be transmitted between two organizations, a transmission mode must be in place. Potential exchange mechanisms between organizations (discussed in greater detail below) include the following:

- **Vicarious experience.** One organization can get information about another by "watching it from afar." This does not require any direct connection between the two groups.

---

[17] Ray Reagans and Bill McEvily, "Network Structure and Knowledge Exchange: The Effects of Cohesion and Range," *Administrative Science Quarterly*, Vol. 48, No. 2, June 2003, pp. 240–267.

[18] Peter Maskell, "Knowledge Creation and Diffusion in Geographic Clusters," *International Journal of Innovation Management*, Vol. 5, No. 2, 2001, pp. 213–237.

[19] Rogers (1995).

[20] Inkpen (1998).

[21] Lane and Lubatkin (1998).

- **Exchange of descriptive information.** Codified knowledge such as manuals, recipes, and instructions can be produced by one group and shared with others. Such exchange modes can be paper or electronic and could be public (e.g., posted on the Internet) or private.
- **Exchange of physical technologies.** Embodied knowledge such as weapons or the materials needed to produce them can be exchanged from one group to another.
- **Direct person-to-person contact.** Actual direct interaction among members of one group with those of another can provide a route for the transmission of knowledge.

Indirect modes of exchange, such as the *vicarious observation* of other group's activities through media reports or public statements, are likely to provide the opportunity for transmission of only small amounts of information. Although such reports can alert groups to the use of particular tactics[22] or potentially promising technologies, research indicates that media reports do not provide sufficient information to replicate them.[23] In comparison, research demonstrates that the *exchange of descriptive information or physical technologies* can be an effective mechanism of technology exchange. But the knowledge needed to use them needs to be codified.[24] For technologies for which all of the required knowledge has not or cannot be codified, success depends on the receiving group being able to "figure out" any of the tacit requirements for using the descriptive information or technology.

Exchanging tacit knowledge requires stronger connections between organizations as well as *direct person-to-person contact.*[25] This

---

[22] For example, media reports of airline hijackings mentioned previously (Holden, 1986).

[23] Rogers (1995).

[24] Joanne Roberts, "From Know-How to Show-How? Questioning the Role of Information and Communications Technologies in Knowledge Exchange," *Technology Analysis and Strategic Management*, Vol. 12, No. 4, 2000, pp. 429–443.

[25] Morten T. Hansen, "The Search-Exchange Problem: The Role of Weak Ties in Sharing Knowledge Across Organizational Subunits," *Administrative Science Quarterly*, Vol. 44, No. 1, 1999, pp. 82–111; Aimée Kane, Linda Argote, and John M. Levine, "Knowledge Exchange Between Groups via Personnel Rotation: Effects of Social Identity and

direct contact allows organizations to address errors in comprehension by the receiving organization, but it also provides the source organization with the opportunity to customize the technology to match the receiving organization's needs. Notably, direct contact can take significant time and effort, especially if receiving organizations require multiple interactions before exchange is effective.[26] This need frequently leads organizations to colocate, increasing the number of interactions.[27]

Since different transmission modes have different strengths from the perspective of explicit and tacit knowledge exchange, organizations frequently combine modes to maximize their chances of success. As a result, regarding technology exchange efforts, the use of multiple media by terrorist groups is of particular concern since combining modes can apply techniques for which each excels; e.g., transmission of instructions or technologies from the source group along with personal contacts can move both the explicit and tacit knowledge needed for effective exchange to the receiver group.

Conclusions

Although the goals and activities of terrorist groups differ from other, nonviolent organizations, previous studies of technology exchange in these nonviolent organizations can provide structures and guidance for assessing terrorist efforts to seek out and obtain new technologies. Both technology diffusion and organizational approaches to technology adoption help to identify a range of variables and issues that could affect terrorist groups' decisions to seek out technology exchange and, more importantly, an approach for assessing their likelihood of being successful. The following chapters bring these insights to bear as part of an assessment of technology exchange among terrorist organizations in three previously described, contemporary cases.

Knowledge Quality," *Organizational Behavior and Human Decision Processes*, Vol. 96, 2005, pp. 56–71.

[26] Eric von Hippel, *The Sources of Innovation*, New York: Oxford University Press, 1988.

[27] Maskell (2001).

CHAPTER THREE

Mindanao: A Mecca for Transnational Terrorism in Southeast Asia

Mindanao, in the southern Philippines, is emerging as one of the most important theaters in the wider global war on terrorism. Long an area of Muslim unrest[1] and rebellion, U.S. security officials have begun to express their concern that local militant groups have been co-opted into a loosely integrated Islamist network. This Islamist network apparently sees its ultimate objective as the creation of a hard-line, fundamentalist, cross-border Caliphate embracing Indonesia, Malaysia, Brunei, Mindanao, and the southern Malay provinces of Thailand. Intelligence officials both internal and external to Southeast Asia now routinely produce threat assessments that pay particularly close attention to the

---

[1] For overviews of the Muslim insurgency in Mindanao, see T. George, *Revolt in Mindanao: The Rise of Islam in Philippine Politics*, Kuala Lumpur: Oxford University Press, 1980; S. Tan, *The Filipino Muslim Struggle 1900–1972*, Manila: Filipinas Foundation, 1977; Mark Turner, "The Management of Violence in a Conflict Organization: The Case of the Abu Sayyaf," *Public Organization Review: A Global Journal*, Vol. 3, No. 4, December 2003, pp. 387–401 [pp. 390–392]; C. Majul, *The Contemporary Muslim Movement in the Philippines*, Berkeley, Calif.: Mizan Press, 1985; R. J. May, "The Wild West in the South: A Recent Political History," in Mark Turner, R. J. May, and L. R. Turner, eds., *Mindanao: Land of Unfulfilled Promise*, Quezon City: New Day Publishers, 1992; Syed Islam, "The Islamic Independence Movement in Pattani of Thailand and Mindanao of the Philippines," *Asian Survey*, Vol. 38, No. 5, 1998; Bgen Ismael Villareal, "Conflict Resolution in Mindanao," *Forum 2*, Summer 1996, pp. 2–11; International Crisis Group (ICG), "Southern Philippines Backgrounder: Terrorism and the Peace Process," *ICG Asia Report No. 80*, Singapore/Brussels, July 13, 2004, pp. 3–5; and Peter Chalk, "The Davao Consensus: A Panacea for the Muslim Insurgency in Mindanao?" *Terrorism and Political Violence*, Vol. 9, No. 2, Summer 1997, pp. 80–82.

attendant nature of operational and logistical links that have emerged between locally based extremists and outside militants.[2]

This chapter examines one element of the Philippine-regional terror nexus: the exchange of explosives technology as well as the knowledge to implement these weapons. To do this, the chapter first discusses the main organizations of concern, concentrating on Jemaah Islamiyah (JI); the Misuari Breakaway Group (MBG) of the Moro National Liberation Front (MNLF); the Abu Sayyaf Group (ASG); the Moro Islamic Liberation Front (MILF); and the Rajah Soliaman Revolutionary Movement (RSRM), a fanatical offshoot of Balik Islam.[3] The chapter then looks at the specific nature of explosive exchanges, the factors that have facilitated this collaboration, and the impact this collaboration is having on the militants' operational tempos.

Background: Islamic Militant Groups in Mindanao

Several groups remain at the forefront of Islamic terrorism in the southern Philippines, including JI, MILF, ASG, MSB-MNLF, and RSRM.

Jemaah Islamiyah (JI)

JI's history dates back to the Darul Islam rebellions[4] that took place in Indonesia during the 1950s, although its organizational inception is generally thought to have occurred in the 1980s when the movement's

---

[2] Personal interviews with intelligence, defense, and security officials, Manila, Bangkok, and Singapore, March–April 2005.

[3] Balik Islam is a movement established in the early 1990s by Ahmed Santos and composed of former Christians who have converted to Islam.

[4] Darul Islam was an Islamic-based guerrilla outfit that fought both the Dutch and the secular-oriented Sukarno regime, arguing that the latter was as much an enemy as the former colonial power. The rebellion lasted until 1962, when its leader was captured and executed. The organization exists to this day and operates in much the same manner as the Muslim Brotherhood in Egypt. See Zachary Abuza, "Al-Qaeda Comes to Southeast Asia," in Paul Smith, ed., *Terrorism and Violence in Southeast Asia: Transnational Challenges to States and Regional Stability*, London: M. E. Sharpe, 2004b, pp. 57–58. For more on the Darul Islam movement, see Adam Schwartz, *A Nation in Waiting: Indonesia in the 1990s*, Boulder, Colo.: Westview Press, 1994, p. 169.

acknowledged founders, Abu Bakar Bashir and Abdullah Sungkar, were exiled to Malaysia. The organization purportedly seeks the creation of pure Islamic communities across Southeast Asia as precursors to the eventual formation of a pan-regional Caliphate—to be known as Darulah Islamiah Raya/Nusantara[5] and embracing Indonesia, Malaysia, Brunei, southern Thailand, and the southern Philippines.[6] JI hopes to achieve this objective through the force of arms, which, over the past four years, has involved several high-profile strikes and attempted assaults, including

- an unsuccessful 2001 plot to carry out a series of coordinated bombings in Singapore targeting U.S. warships docked at the Changi Naval Base, the Ministry of Defense, a shuttle bus serving the Sembawang Wharves and Yishun subway, the U.S. and Israeli embassies, the British and Australian high commissions, and commercial complexes housing Western business interests[7]
- the 2002 Bali attack, which resulted in 202 fatalities and which remains the most destructive act of international terrorism since 9/11
- the 2003 suicide attack against the U.S.-owned Marriott Hotel in Jakarta, which left 13 people dead and dozens injured
- the 2004 bombing of the Australian embassy in Jakarta, which caused extensive structural damage to the building as well as numerous casualties[8]

---

[5] Unified Islamic Republic or Caliphate.

[6] Peter Chalk, "Militant Islamic Extremism in Southeast Asia," in Paul Smith, ed., *Terrorism and Violence in Southeast Asia: Transnational Challenges to States and Regional Stability*, London: M. E. Sharpe, 2004, pp. 19–37 [p. 27]; Abuza (2004b, pp. 43–44). See also ICG, "Al-Qaeda in Southeast Asia: The Case of the 'Ngruki' Network in Indonesia," *Asia Briefing No. 20*, Jakarta/Brussels, August 8, 2002; and ICG, "Jemaah Islamiyah in Southeast Asia: Damaged but Still Dangerous," *Asia Report No. 63*, Jakarta/Brussels, August 26, 2003.

[7] The plot to attack these high-profile venues was uncovered when U.S. Special Forces discovered reconnaissance videos of Singapore in the ruins of post-Taliban Afghanistan. See Stephen Ulph, "Continuing JI Concerns in Singapore," *Terrorism Focus*, Vol. 2, No. 8, April 28, 2005a.

[8] Chalk (2005, pp. 28–29).

- the 2004 bombing of Philippine *SuperFerry 14*, a coordinated operation with the RSRM and ASG that resulted in 116 fatalities (discussed below)[9]
- the 2005 Valentine's Day bombings in Manila, Davao, and General Santos City, another joint operation with ASG and RSRM that left 12 people dead and more than 140 injured (discussed below)[10]
- an alleged 2005 plan to target venues in Manila's central business district popular with Western tourists as well as mass and light rail transit tracks and stations; this was yet another plot that Philippine intelligence sources believe was to have involved elements from RSRM and ASG (discussed below).[11]

Operationally, JI—at least initially—was thought to work in much the same networked manner as al Qaeda, comprising (1) an Indonesia-based central command (*qiyadah maraziyah*, which is part of a wider governing council, the *majelis qiyadah*); (2) a hard core of dedicated militants; and (3) a wider associate base drawn both from established militant groups and from loosely based radicals scattered across the region. A 2003 white paper prepared by the Singapore government claimed these cadres, the numbers of which vary greatly by

---

[9] Personal interview with Maritime Intelligence Group (MIG) official, Washington D.C., August 2005, and the Anti-Terrorism Task Force (ATTF), Manila, November 2005.

[10] Personal interviews with counterterrorism and intelligence officials, Manila, March and November 2005. See also "Over 60 Hurt in Makati Explosion; GMA Inspects Site," *ABS-CBN News*, February 14, 2005; "Bombs in 3 Cities Kill 6," *The New York Times*, February 15, 2005; and "4 More Suspects in V-Day Bombings Nabbed," *ABS-CBN News*, February 23, 2005.

[11] Interviews with Philippine and Singaporean antiterrorism and intelligence officials, Manila and Singapore, March and November 2005. See also Donna Pazzibugan, "10 Sacks of Explosives Seized," *The Philippine Daily Inquirer*, March 24, 2005; Tarra Quismundo and Donna Pazzibugan, "Bomb Found Outside Makati Bldg.," *The Philippine Daily Inquirer*, March 28, 2005; and "JI Linking with Other Terror Groups, Singapore Warns," *The Philippine Daily Inquirer*, March 30, 2005.

source,[12] were organized into specific territorial cells known as *mantiqis* covering the following areas:

- M1—Singapore, Malaysia (except Sabah), and southern Thailand
- M2—Indonesia (except Sulawesi and Kalimantan)
- M3—Sabah, Sulawesi, Kalimantan, and the southern Philippines
- M4—Australia and Papua New Guinea.[13]

Thanks to a concerted crackdown on JI by regional police, the military, and intelligence authorities, especially in Malaysia and Singapore, it is unlikely that this hierarchical structure continues to hold today. Most commentators concur that, while Indonesia probably continues to constitute the main center of gravity, the group has assumed a far flatter character (in common with al Qaeda) with the bulk of its attacks now farmed out to like-minded radicals who operate on a semi- (if not fully) autonomous basis. These same observers further assert that due to the reduced "militant space" available in Southeast Asia, the crux of JI mission-oriented and logistical activities has narrowed to two main zones: southern Thailand[14] and, especially, the southern

---

[12] JI's total membership has never been established, with estimates ranging from a few hundred to several thousand. According to Singaporean authorities, active operational cadres today probably number between 500 and 700, the bulk of whom are thought to be in Indonesia (author interview, Security Intelligence Directorate, Ministry of Defense, Singapore, April 2005). See also Abuza (2004b, p. 44) and Government of the Republic of Indonesia, *Indictment of Abu Bakar Bashir*, Jakarta: Office of the Attorney General, April 2003.

[13] Singapore Ministry of Home Affairs, *The Jemaah Islamiyah Arrests and the Threat of Terrorism: White Paper*, Singapore: Ministry of Home Affairs, Republic of Singapore, 2003, p. 10. See also Richard Evans, "Singapore Reports on Jemaah Islamiah," *Jane's Intelligence Review*, February 2003; and "Singapore Offers Grim View of Future Terror," *The Sydney Morning Herald* (Australia), January 11–12, 2003.

[14] The main area of concern in Thailand focuses on the southern Malay provinces of Narithiwat, Yala, and Pattani. Over the last two years, the scale of unrest perpetrated by local separatist groups has risen markedly, taking on a far more open-ended, civilian-centric character. Moreover, in April 2005, a series of attacks took place against the French-owned supermarket chain Carrefour and the international airport in Hat Yai. These were the first instances of violence in the south taking on a specific, anti-Western (or at least non–Thai-centric) focus.

Philippines. According to various sources in Singapore, affiliates in the latter theater presently constitute the primary conduit through which the movement seeks to achieve its regional objectives.[15]

Moro Islamic Liberation Front (MILF)

The MILF emerged from a 1977 rift within the larger MNLF.[16] MILF's avowed objective is the creation of a sovereign Islamic state, to be governed by sharia law, in all areas where Muslims have traditionally existed as a majority in the southern Philippines. Despite the common emphasis on religion and independence, MILF is acknowledged to be infused with a more tolerant ideology than the ASG and generally does not subscribe to the latter's wholesale rejection of religious cohabitation.

The MILF is, by far, the strongest group currently operating in Mindanao. The organization is able to call on a committed core of between 15,000 and 20,000 cadres (more if irregular or part-time fighters are included),[17] a wider passive support base of several thousand, and an impressive inventory of weapons that includes new M-16s, ArmaLites® (many with grenade launchers), RPG-2s, B-40 rocket launchers, .45-caliber pistols, machine and antiaircraft guns, and a variety of small and medium mortars.[18] Having said that, the MILF is probably weaker today than at any time in the past, largely as a result of various territorial defeats suffered at the hands of the Philippine

---

Several commentators in Bangkok believe that these trends are possibly indicative of growing JI influence in this part of the country (personal interviews with journalists and Western diplomatic officials, Bangkok, March–April 2005).

[15] Personal interviews with security analysts and intelligence officials, Singapore, April 2005.

[16] The MILF split from the MNLF after the latter signed on to the Tripoli Agreement in 1976, which affirmed autonomy rather than full independence for Mindanao. For an overview of the agreement and the reasons for its failure, see Villareal (1996) and Chalk (1997).

[17] The MILF is divided into nine base commands, each of which is comprised of individual unit brigades.

[18] Zachary Abuza, "The Moro Islamic Liberation Front at 20: State of the Revolution," paper prepared for the NIC-State/INR/EAT Conference on Mindanao, Washington, D.C., July 9, 2004a, pp. 3–5, 10–13.

army. These defeats include, most notably, the capture of its main base at Camp Abu Bakar as-Siddique in 2000 and the loss of the Buliok Complex (which had been developed as an alternative headquarters) in 2003.[19]

Possibly as a result of this weakened state, the MILF has been prepared to engage in tentative peace talks with the Philippine government, which, for its part, appears to have accepted that the Moro insurgency does not lend itself to a purely military solution.[20] This dialogue has progressed rapidly over the last couple of years, facilitated in large part by the death of hard-line MILF founder Hashim Salamat[21] and his replacement with the more pragmatic Haji Murad (MILF's former spokesperson). Significantly, the new leader has expressed a willingness to revisit the issue of secession, hinting that he may be willing to drop the demand for independence if a genuine level of autonomy is granted to Mindanao.[22] At the time of writing, a general cessation of hostilities was holding between Manila and the MILF (embracing a guarantee that all existing MILF bases will remain off-limits to army incursions), with the two sides participating in a fresh round of negotiations brokered by Malaysia.[23]

Although welcome, Murad's willingness to deal with the administration of President Gloria Macapagal-Arroyo on a diplomatic level

---

[19] See, for instance, Anthony Davis, "Philippine Army Prevents MILF Reorganisation," *Jane's Intelligence Review*, March 2003a, pp. 16–21; Anthony Davis, "Attention Shifts to Moro Islamic Liberation Front," *Jane's Intelligence Review*, April 2002, pp. 20–22; "Philippine Forces Hit Rebel Stronghold," *The Washington Post*, April 24, 2000; Rajiv Chandrasekaran, "Philippine Troops Fire at Rebel Camp," *The Washington Post*, May 8, 2000c; "Philippines Seizes Rebel Headquarters," *The Washington Post*, July 10, 2000; "War Without End," *The Economist*, May 3, 2003; and "Philippine Government Calls Off Peace Moves," *Japan Today*, May 6, 2003.

[20] In addition, the Arroyo administration is keen to consolidate a peace agreement with MILF to free up military resources to deal with renewed unrest and political violence emanating from the 8,000-strong New People's Army, the armed wing of the Communist Party of the Philippines (personal interviews, Manila, March 2005).

[21] Salamat died of natural causes in mid-2003.

[22] Personal interviews with Western diplomats and journalists, Manila, Bangkok, and Singapore, March–April 2005.

[23] "Manila and Rebels Reach Agreement," *BBC News*, April 20, 2005.

has complicated the internal dynamics of MILF. While the group's leadership and mainstream do seem sincere in their desire for peace, several mid-level field officers have vociferously denounced the present negotiations as a capitulation to the dictates of Manila and as tantamount to the wholesale betrayal of the Moro Islamic cause. These so-called "lost commands," many of which enjoy a substantial degree of operational latitude on a day-to-day basis, have vowed to continue the armed struggle for independence irrespective of any accord between the MILF Central Committee and Manila.[24] It is these renegade blocs that most commentators believe are at the forefront of continuing unrest in Mindanao, reputedly working in collaboration both with other domestic extremists as well as outside jihadists connected to JI.[25]

Abu Sayyaf Group (ASG)

ASG was founded in 1989 under the leadership of Ustadz Abdurajak Janjalini, a former member of the Filipino Muslim Brigade who went to fight Soviet occupation forces in Afghanistan. At its inception, the group styled itself as a fundamentalist jihadist group committed to the establishment of an exclusive, independent Islamic State of Mindanao and the eradication of all Christian influence in the southern Philippines. Almost immediately, the group moved to establish ties with outside extremist elements, emerging as a key player in the so-called *Bojinka* Plots that aimed to (1) target U.S. embassies in Manila and Bangkok; (2) assassinate the Pope and President Clinton during separate visits to the Philippines between 1995 and 1996; and (3) destroy 11 U.S. commercial airliners flying trans-Pacific routes from West Coast cities. The plan was hatched by Ramzi Yousef—the convicted mastermind of the 1993 attack on the World Trade Center in

---

[24] Important in this regard are Jack Abdullah, Gordon Saifullah, and Amelil Umbra, the respective leaders of MILF's 105th, 101st, and 109th Base Commands. See ICG (2004, p. 10).

[25] Personal interviews with Philippine police and military intelligence and Western diplomatic officials, Manila, March 2005.

New York—and was foiled only when volatile explosive compounds caught fire in the apartment that he was renting in Manila.[26]

In 1998, Janjalini was killed during a shoot-out with Philippine police, after which the ASG degenerated into a loose collection of bandits and warlords motivated less by ideology and self-defined religious piousness than pure financial gain and greed.[27] The group's structure has further atrophied by sustained assaults on its traditional strongholds in the Sulu Sea—Basilan and Jolo—since 2002, which have successfully reduced overall ASG numbers to around 100–200 cadres, a substantial reduction from the roughly 1,100 militants who had made up the organization's (unified) membership in 1999.[28]

---

[26] Chalk (2004, pp. 20–21); Abuza (2004b, p. 42); Mark Turner, "Terrorism and Secession in the Southern Philippines: The Rise of the Abu Sayyaf," *Contemporary Southeast Asia*, Vol. 17, No. 1, June 1995, pp. 1–18; Turner (2003, pp. 395–396); "Validation of the Existence of the ASG," internal document prepared for the Philippine National Intelligence Coordinating Agency (NICA), February 14, 1997; International Institute for Strategic Studies (IISS), "Separatist Rebellion in the Southern Philippines," *Strategic Comments*, Vol. 6, No. 4, May 2000, p. 4; Simon Elegant, "Asia's Own Osama," *Time Magazine*, April 1, 2002; Anthony Spaeth, "Rumbles in the Jungle," *Time Magazine*, March 4, 2002; "Disparate Pieces of Terrorism Puzzle Fit Together," *The Washington Post*, September 23, 2001; "Muslim Militants Threaten Ramos Vision of Summit Glory," *The Australian*, January 13, 1996; and "Clinton Kill Plot Claim," *The Courier-Mail* (Australia), May 22, 1996. According to Rohan Gunaratna, had Operation Bojinka taken place, more than 4,000 civilians would have been collectively killed (comments made during the Globalising Terror, Political Violence in the New Millennium Conference, Hobart, Tasmania, May 8–10, 2002).

[27] Between 1999 and 2004, the bulk of ASG activities took the form of kidnappings, some of which were highly profitable. A string of Western abductions carried out in the first half of 2000, for instance, are believed to have netted an estimated $20 million in ransom payments. See Turner (2003, pp. 389–390); "A Hostage Crisis Confronts Estrada," *The Economist*, May 6, 2000; "Philippine Forces Hit Rebel Stronghold" (2000); Rajiv Chandrasekaran, "Gunmen Take Foreigners Hostage in Malaysia," *The Washington Post*, April 25, 2000a; Rajiv Chandrasekaran, "Military Finds Two Beheaded by Philippine Rebels," *The Washington Post*, May 7, 2000b; "Libya Denies Ransom Offer for Hostages," *The Sacramento Bee*, August 13, 2000; and "No More Ransoms," *The Economist*, June 2, 2001.

[28] Personal interviews with police and military intelligence officials, Manila, March 2005. See also Chalk (2004, p. 21); Anthony Davis, "Resilient Abu Sayyaf Resists Military Pressure," *Jane's Intelligence Review*, September 1, 2003b, p. 17; and Anthony Davis, "Philippines Fears New Wave of Attacks by Abu Sayyaf Group," *Jane's Intelligence Review*, May 1, 2005, p. 11.

Having said that, there does appear to have been an attempt to reenergize the ASG as a credible and integrated Islamic force since roughly mid-2004. According to Philippine and Singaporean intelligence sources, much of this effort is being directed under the combined auspices of Khaddafy Janjalini (the younger brother of Abdurajak Janjalini) and Jainal Antel Sali (aka Abu Soleiman, a principal ASG spokesman), who have emerged as key leaders of the group thanks to the death of several competing "commanders" during an attempted jailbreak in March 2005.[29] In April, Khaddafy, who had been mistakenly reported killed following a military air strike in November 2004, issued a statement that he was alive and was preparing for a renewed offensive against the Philippine state. Moreover, he affirmed that, henceforth, the ASG would be known as the Al-Harakat-ul-Al-Islamiya,[30] a nomenclature that several commentators in Southeast Asia view as indicative of a reoriented tactical and operational agenda toward a more explicit jihadist focus.[31]

Misuari Breakaway Group (MBG-MNLF) and the Rajah Soliaman Revolutionary Movement (RSRM)

The MBG-MNLF and RSRM are two relative newcomers to the conflict in the southern Philippines. The former is a breakaway faction of the MNLF,[32] which originally signed a peace agreement with Manila

---

[29] These included Alhamser Manatad Limbong (alias Commander Kosovo), Ghalib Andang (alias Commander Robot), and Nadjul Sabdula (alias Commander Global). At the time of this writing, there existed only one competing ASG band challenging the leadership of Janjalini: a faction under the control of Isnilon Hapilon in the southern coastal Sultan Kudarat district.

[30] Islamic movement.

[31] Personal interviews with police and military intelligence officials, Manila and Singapore, March–April 2005. See also Arlyn de la Cruz, "Janjalini Alive, Vows to Avenge Abu Jail Deaths," *The Philippine Daily Inquirer,* April 2, 2005; and Davis (2005, pp. 10–11).

[32] The MNLF traditionally served as the main vehicle for the Muslim insurgency in Mindanao. The organization was created in 1971 under the leadership of Nur Misuari and, through its military wing, the Bangsa Moro Army, fought a protracted battle for Mindanao's independence that, over the course of 25 years, resulted in massive physical damage, a growing refugee problem, and a death toll in the hundreds of thousands.

in 1996 (the Davao Consensus).[33] The group is primarily composed of fighters who have become disillusioned with the peace dividend in Mindanao and who took to arms following the 2002 arrest of Nur Misuari, the original founder of the MNLF, on charges that he incited a rebellion in November 2001 that left more than 100 people dead in Jolo and Zamboanga City.[34] The MBG has since been implicated in several large clashes with security forces in the southern Philippines and is widely believed to operate in conjunction with the ASG and lost commands of the MILF.[35]

The RSRM is a highly fanatical fringe element of Balik Islam (literally "return to Islam").[36] Little publicly available information exists on the RSRM, although a recent Philippine intelligence assessment postulates that the group was established in 2002 with the goal of establishing a theocratic Islamic state across the entire country, supposedly to rectify the artificial influx of Catholic influence that was

---

[33] The 1996 agreement provided for the creation of two main bodies: (1) an Autonomous Region of Muslim Mindanao (ARMM) covering five provinces that had limited powers of local governance over the extraction of resources, education, religion, and the administration of justice; and (2) a Southern Philippine Council for Peace and Development (SPCPD) to oversee social and economic development in all provinces and cities with a majority Muslim population (an area that is composed of roughly 10 million inhabitants, which represents approximately 55 percent of the 18 million people in Mindanao's total population). For an overview of the agreement, see Chalk (1997).

[34] Although Misuari was integral to the 1996 peace agreement with Manila and elected as the governor of ARMM as well as the chairman of the SPCPD, the MNLF's Central Committee (the organization's highest policymaking body) removed him from both posts in August 2001 for general ineptitude and corruption. Following his disposition, Misuari declared his opposition to the Davao Consensus and took up arms against Manila with 200 followers. After the November encounters with the military, he fled to Malaysia where he was captured and deported back to the Philippines. He is currently being held at Fort Santo Domingo, Santa Rosa—the same prison in which former President "Erap" Estrada is incarcerated. See "The Jolo Conundrum," *The Economist*, November 24, 2001; Christine Herrera, "Misuari Failed to Deliver–OIC," *The Philippine Daily Inquirer*, January 2, 2002; and "Fighting Rages in Jolo," *Filipinoexpress.com*, February 10, 2005.

[35] Personal interviews with military and police intelligence officials, Manila, March 2005.

[36] The Philippine Office of Muslim Affairs estimates that Balik Islam currently boasts a membership of some 200,000 converts (or "reverts" as they prefer to be called). See Johnna Villaviray, "When Christians Embrace Islam," *The Manila Times*, November 17, 2003.

first introduced by the Spanish and then consolidated under the U.S. protectorate. The report alleges that the group has a special action force for carrying out urban attacks and is financed by money from Saudi Arabia channeled through various Islamic charities based in the Philippines. According to the analysis, the RSRM focuses on converting Christians to Islam and then presses them to convert to a militant form of Islam that advocates the violent concept of jihad.[37]

Like the MBG-MNLF and renegade factions of the MILF, the RSRM is believed to act in coordination with the ASG, reputedly receiving $200,000 from Khaddafy Janjalini in 2004 to carry out terrorist strikes in Manila. Although the RSRM is small, even relative to the ASG, Western and Philippine security officials remain concerned about the potential threat posed by its members for two main reasons: first, their intimate knowledge of operational theaters outside Mindanao;[38] and second, the possibility that they are more predisposed to mass, indiscriminate murder as a means of demonstrating their Islamic credentials.[39]

Rationalizing the Exchange of Technology and Knowledge

There are several interrelated reasons for JI being prepared to exchange explosive weapon technology with Islamist groups in the southern Philippines and for these organizations seeking to obtain such expertise.

JI Rationale

For the leaders of JI, three main factors have been apparent. First, the group has been actively interested in availing itself of MILF camps,

---

[37] See "Summary of Report," *The Manila Times*, April 12, 2004.

[38] According to Philippine authorities, at least 20 percent of Balik Islam members live in the northern Luzon region of the Philippines, which includes some of the country's largest cities.

[39] Personal interviews with Philippine intelligence and Western diplomatic officials, Manila, March 2005. See also Davis (2005, p. 12).

which, as noted above, remain essentially immune from military offensives. This has arguably made Filipino bases more secure than those in Indonesia—particularly in light of the intense regional and international pressure Jakarta has faced to intensify its counterterrorism efforts over the last several years—as well as helped to foster the type of guarded territorial haven that is so crucial for the successful planning and execution of long-range strategic attacks. Regional commentators generally agree that JI has sought to use provision of explosive (and other) training as a lever for gaining guaranteed access to these advantageous facilities.[40]

Second, there are strong reasons to believe that JI wishes to transform the Philippines into an attack as well as a logistical theater. The Republic's overwhelming Catholic character, its universal endorsement of capitalism and liberal democracy, and Manila's own strong defense relationship with the United States (which has included sending military units to Iraq) all symbolize much of what the Salafi Jihadi movement actively opposes. Moreover, because there is not a sizable Muslim presence outside Mindanao, there is far greater functional latitude for carrying out assaults that are unlikely to impact on wider Islamist interests. Empowering locally based groups to undertake concerted strikes in cities such as Manila provides JI with a conduit through which to perpetrate large-scale acts of civilian-centric violence and, thereby, operationalize a new hub for transregional militant extremism.[41]

Third, and directly related to the above two points, it would be difficult for JI to act independently in the Philippines given the enormous ethnic and linguistic diversity that exists across the Republic. According to one defense official, because people look, eat, and speak differently from one province to the next, outsiders attempting to infiltrate and operate under their own auspices in local communities would almost certainly stand out and be quickly exposed.[42] Govern-

---

[40] Personal interviews with intelligence officials, security analysts, and journalists, Honolulu, Manila, Bangkok, and Singapore, March–April 2005.

[41] Briefing to author from Security Intelligence Directorate (SID), Singapore, April 2005.

[42] Indeed, the capture of Zaki in March 2005 resulted primarily from suspicion aroused by his poor understanding of Tagalog (the national language) and apparent lack of understand-

ment sources in Manila contend that JI readily appreciates this reality, arguing that, as a result, the movement has been forced to extend its operational and logistical presence in the country primarily by working through "home-grown militants that are both known and trusted in their respective regions."[43]

Filipino Islamist Rationale

Filipino Islamists have been interested in working with JI for similarly self-interested, pragmatic reasons. These organizations are keen to access the latter's expertise in order to augment their own operational tempos and expand attack platforms to areas beyond the southern Mindanao theater. More specifically, by successfully striking out and destroying targets in the heartland of the Philippine state, including the capital, groups such as ASG and MILF are able to demonstrate their durability as a meaningful force and concept, establishing a benchmark of power that can then be used to build morale and attract new recruits.[44]

Just as important, working with JI—widely regarded as the most dangerous terrorist organization operating in Southeast Asia—is deemed an effective means of validating the wider jihadist "credentials" of the southern Filipino struggle for independence. This issue of credibility is especially relevant to the ASG: It has sought to recast itself from a bandit kidnap-for-ransom outfit to a bona fide religious insurgency.[45] *Jane's* defense analyst Anthony Davis observes,

> [T]he last two years have seen a new and disturbing shift towards ideologically inspired, high-profile attacks that parallels the ASG's

---

ing of local Maguindanao customs and traditions.

[43] Personal interviews with U.S. Department of Defense officials, Manila, March 31, 2005.

[44] Personal interviews with intelligence officials, Manila and Singapore, March–April 2005.

[45] Personal interviews with intelligence officials and analysts, Honolulu and Manila, March 2005.

growing interaction with JI. . . . At the same time . . . kidnappings for ransom have virtually ceased.[46]

Finally, it is likely that MILF lost commands have actively sought to consolidate ties with JI as a fallback position in the event that the organization's political leadership negotiates a peace deal with Manila.[47] Should Murad sign an agreement with the Arroyo administration, not only would the army have greater latitude to deal with rejectionist elements in the south (as human and material resources would be freed up and extant limits on raids would no longer hold), the MILF itself could take action against destabilizing holdout elements.

Identifying Exchanges in Mindanao

To complicate matters, organizational lines between the various militant Muslim groups operating in the southern Philippines have blurred. As one commentator put it: "One can be a member of ASG on Monday, the MILF on Tuesday, RSRM on Wednesday, and the MGB on Thursday."[48] It is, therefore, more useful to concentrate on the general Islamic extremist milieu in Mindanao as opposed to specific groups per se. Within this context, the main collaboration that appears to have taken place focuses on explosives technology, especially with regard to constructing bombs that are more powerful and reliable.

In the past, most attacks associated with southern Filipino extremists involved rudimentary improvised explosive devices (IEDs), constructed from dynamite sticks and blasting caps stolen from locally based mining and fishing companies. In most cases, militants detonated these bombs using a simple delayed timer switch linked to and activated by a basic analog alarm clock (usually Chinese-made).[49]

---

[46] Davis (2005, p. 12).

[47] Personal interview with military intelligence officials, Manila, March 2005.

[48] Personal interview with police intelligence officials, Manila, March 2005.

[49] Personal interviews with Western diplomats and military intelligence officials, Manila, March 2005.

Although these devices successfully caused localized damage, they were never able to deliver the type of crushing explosive force necessary for more widespread destruction. Moreover, on several occasions, the bombs went off early, late, or not at all, as a result of faulty triggering mechanisms.[50]

Over the last several years, however, the nature and sophistication of IEDs employed by southern Filipino Islamists has changed. Today, the typical device is made from either converted field ordnance (such as 60-mm mortar shells or rocket-propelled grenades) or C4 plastic explosives,[51] combined with a potassium chlorate/ammonium nitrate mixture and then linked to a TNT booster charge that is remotely detonated using a cell phone.[52] Not only has the blast radius of these weapons proven to be far greater than the traditional dynamite and ordnance bomb, the introduction of cellular technology has been instrumental in reducing the incidence of failed and mistimed detonations as well as ensuring for a greater body count (largely because IEDs can be detonated in line of sight of a specific target at a specific time).

Certain highly specialized bomb-making and concealment techniques have also become apparent. In February 2005, an IED recovered in Cotabato City contained a secondary, pressure-activated switch that appears to have been designed to trigger an automatic detonation in the event that security authorities attempted to move or defuse it.[53] A month later, an enormous cache of explosives was discovered in Manila, allegedly stockpiled in preparation for attacks in the central business district of Makati.[54] Notably, the consignment included

---

[50] Personal interview with Western diplomatic official, Manila, March 2005.

[51] In some instances, these IEDs have used a commercially available emulsion plastic explosive known as Powergel. Powergel® is a registered trademark of Indian Explosives Limited.

[52] Personal interviews with military and intelligence officials, Manila and Singapore, March–April 2005.

[53] Personal interview with Western diplomat, Manila, March 2005.

[54] Personal interview with military intelligence officials, Manila, March 2005. See also Pazzibugan (2005); "JI Linking with Other Terror Groups, Singapore Warns," *The Philippine Daily Inquirer*, March 30, 2005; and "Car Bombing Plot Foiled, Says AFP," *The Philippine Daily Inquirer*, March 30, 2005.

C4 compounds that were hidden in toothpaste tubes, deodorant cans, shampoo bottles, and film canisters. As one Bangkok-based journalist put it, "This is sophisticated stuff and certainly not something that you would typically associate with run-of-the mill Philippine terrorism."[55]

Most regional commentators concur that the increased visibility of these more advanced technologies reflects JI training and expertise. Not only is the group known to have accessed MILF base camps in the past,[56] the specific makeup of IEDs that have surfaced over the last several years have a distinctly external "handprint" to them:

- The construction of bombs made from a mixture of C4, potassium chlorate/ammonium nitrate, and TNT closely resemble the type of devices routinely used in Indonesia.[57]
- The employment of cell phones to detonate IEDs remotely is a signature trait of JI.
- Most of the cell phones recovered from southern Filipino Islamists are the same Nokia® 3310 models that have been used to conduct large-scale attacks in cities such as Jakarta.
- The pressure-activated bomb discovered in 2005 is reminiscent of the devices used in Afghanistan—a theater that is known to have formed the crux of JI's early training and experience in weapon technology.[58]

Philippine officials further contend that JI's influence is evident in the manner by which attacks are now being executed in the country. Increasingly, strikes are taking the form of synchronized, coordinated attacks aimed at maximizing collateral damage. The 2005 Valentine's Day bombings are singled out as a case in point. Widely believed to

---

[55] Personal interview with journalist, Bangkok, April 2005. See also Davis (2005, p. 12).

[56] The ICG has published several comprehensive reports detailing past JI-MILF links. See, especially, ICG (2002, 2003, 2004). See also Abuza (2004a).

[57] Potassium chlorate, for instance, was one of the main compounds used in the 2002 Bali bombings.

[58] Personal interviews with police and military intelligence, Western diplomats, and journalists, Manila, Bangkok, and Singapore, March–April 2005.

have been a joint ASG-JI-RSRM venture, the operation involved three explosions that took place within 30 minutes of each other: two in the southern cities of Davao and General Santos and one in the business district of Manila. As noted above, 12 people were killed and more than 140 injured in the triple strikes, with the capital incident clearly designed to cause significant casualties: The explosion took place at a busy intersection that lies adjacent to several major bus stops as well as a heavily used mass rail transit terminal. As Davis points out,

> The bombings reflected a capacity for [thorough surveillance and] carefully coordinated, near simultaneous strikes that has not been typical of ASG operations in the past and may well reflect JI's modus operandi.[59]

The March 2005 attack purportedly planned for Makati (see above) also is singled out as evidentiary of a JI influence. In this instance, the target was a nightclub popular with Western tourists. Military intelligence sources believe that the attack was going to be modeled along the lines of the 2002 Bali atrocity, pointing out that, had it occurred, it would have represented a first in at least two respects: (1) the first specific use of a vehicle to carry out a bombing and (2) the first time an attack venue was deliberately singled out on account of its foreign national association.[60]

A third commonly cited example concerns the bombing of *Super-Ferry 14* on February 27, 2004. Philippine intelligence officials believe that the mechanics for this operation were put together by the ASG with JI backing and then executed using an RSRM cadre. The focus on a passenger ship has caused particular consternation, not least because these targets are relatively easy to hit in a manner that is likely to elicit a large body count. While the exact intent of the attack continues to be a matter of debate,[61] 116 people were killed in the incident, the major-

---

[59] Davis (2005, p. 12).

[60] Personal interviews with police and military intelligence officials, Manila, March 2005.

[61] Several commentators have cast doubt on the intent of this particular operation, observing that the bomb used in the attack exploded in a passenger sleeping berth and involved only 20 sticks of dynamite (which were hidden in a hollowed-out television set). Neither

ity of whom perished when the ship capsized in the Bay of Manila after being towed back to shore.[62]

Significantly, Manila contends that these cases are reflective of a wider, more generalized trend in rising attack tempos that is being fed and directed by outside JI militants. The major fear is that exchanges of explosive weapon technology from outside groups are not only availing greater latitude for actually conducting large-scale bombings but, more intrinsically, are "positively" impacting the perceived cost-benefit calculation of engaging in such acts in the first place. Moreover, there is at least a residual concern among certain commentators that this escalatory spiral will eventually culminate in a decision to carry out suicide strikes, which, even if executed on an irregular, sporadic basis, would fundamentally transform the operational context of the contemporary Filipino terrorist environment.[63]

In addition to detonation technologies and attack patterns, the existence of a JI presence has been identified in the guise of bomb-makers who are either known or suspected to be working in collaboration with Filipino Islamists. Officials with Manila's Anti-Terrorism Task Force estimate that between 30 and 40 JI trainers are currently scattered across the south, notably in various regions around renegade

---

the placement nor the size of this payload is consistent with the objective of destroying a ship (detonating a car or truck bomb beneath the vessel's waterline would have been far more effective) and, indeed, the *SuperFerry 14* was towed for three hours before it listed and sunk. Western diplomats as well as a number of Philippine antiterrorism intelligence officials speculate that the real purpose of the attack could have been to coerce money from the company that owned the vessel (which had been the subject of various earlier extortion threats) (personal interviews with officials from the Anti-Terrorism Task Force [ATTF] in Manila, March 2005).

[62] Personal interviews with police, intelligence, and defense officials and security analysts, Manila and Singapore, March–April 2005. See also Davis (2005, p. 12). The initial blast did not destroy the ferry (see above); however, the explosion did trigger a major fire that could not be contained due to the ferry's faulty sprinkler system. Tugs towed the vessel back to Manila where it eventually capsized—some three hours after the explosion first took place.

[63] Personal interviews with Western diplomats and security analysts, Manila and Singapore, March–April 2005. It should be noted that Philippine intelligence sources tend to downplay the possibility of suicide strikes, arguing that martyrdom is simply not something in the Filipino psyche. That said, they do affirm that southern Islamists would probably have no hesitation in assisting with the logistics of a suicide attack undertaken by an outsider.

MILF base commands.[64] These operatives are thought to include explosive specialists Dulmatin and Abdul Patek; brothers Abdul Rahman Ayub and Abdul Rahim Ayub; and Noordin Mohammad Top, a Malaysian who has been the subject of intensive police investigations over the last few years. It is hoped that the March 2005 capture of Zaki (aka "Rohmat"), a prominent Indonesian explosives instructor, in the Maguindanao province of south-central Mindanao, will shed further light on JI's links with local groups and the extent to which the movement is exchanging weapon technology and expertise.[65]

Contextualizing the Exchanges

Several factors have facilitated the exchanges of explosives technology between JI and Islamist extremists in the southern Philippines. Porous borders have been particularly important, allowing outside radicals to cross illegally from Malaysia and Indonesia with very little risk of detection or interception.[66] Much of the situation derives from the under-

---

[64] Personal interview with defense and intelligence officials, Manila, March 2005. See also Stephen Ulph, "Peace Talks Amid Renewed Violence in the Philippines," *Terrorism Focus*, Vol. 2, No. 8, April 28, 2005b.

[65] Zaki is thought to be a main link between JI and ASG and has been directly connected to the 2004 attack against *SuperFerry 14* as well as the Valentine's Day bombings and alleged Makati attack in 2005. He has asserted that several JI instructors are presently in the southern Philippines and are actively facilitating with preparations for further attacks against strategic targets in the country. Notably, he has claimed that he was dispatched to the southern Philippines to undertake a commercial diving course at a resort located on Palawan island. This has raised concern that JI may be seeking to work with local groups to carry out underwater attacks, possibly against natural gas and oil pipelines located off the southern Philippine seaboard (personal interviews with intelligence officials, Manila and Singapore, March–April 2005). See also Davis (2005, p. 11); Jeff Antiporda and Anthony Vargas, "Terrorist Trainer Nabbed," *The Manila Times*, March 23, 2005; Jim Gomez, "Suspect Says Terrorists Being Trained," *The Star-Bulletin* (Honolulu), March 24, 2005; "Abu Sayyaf Guerrillas Training for Sea-Borne Terror Attacks," *The Khaleej Times*, March 17, 2005; and "Terrorists Train for Seaborne Attacks," Associated Press, March 18, 2005.

[66] Personal interview with military and police intelligence officials, Manila, March 2005. At the time of writing, it was estimated that between 10,000 and 15,000 undocumented Indonesians were living in Mindanao.

resourced and antiquated nature of Manila's navy, which is unable to mount an effective and sustained regime of coastal surveillance in the waters around Mindanao, the Zamboanga peninsula, and the outlying islands of Basilan, Jolo, and Tawi-Tawi.[67] The resulting maritime void has been deftly exploited by JI affiliates, who according to local commentators are believed to enter the Philippines via one of three primary "backdoor" routes:

- from Sabah to Zamboanga and then Cotabato City (primary Malaysian route, which takes about 10 hours)
- from Sandahan to Jolo and then Cotabato City (alternative Malaysian route)
- from Manado to General Santos City (primary Indonesian route)
- from Sulawesi to the Sarangani coastline of southern Mindanao (alternative Indonesian route).[68]

In addition, there is a long history of interaction between Islamist groups in the southern Philippines. This has provided an appropriate organizational framework through which to establish and consolidate links with outside groups such as JI. The fact that many members of the MNLF, ASG, and MILF participated in the anti-Soviet mujahideen campaign during the 1980s has further encouraged these ties, not least by making these cadres receptive and open to the concept of jihad as well as the existence of a wider Islamist fraternity—predicated on a communal tradition of "hospitality"—that makes no distinction between Muslims on a national basis.[69]

Besides these considerations, the southern Philippine region offers a highly conducive environment in which to act. Unlike Malaysia and

---

[67] Defense officials generally lament the poor state of surveillance along the southern Philippine coastal frontier, citing shortages of coastal and airborne monitoring craft, immigration personnel, computerized entry-exit procedures, and networked communication systems.

[68] Personal interview with security analyst, Singapore, April 2005. See also Davis (2005, p. 11).

[69] Personal interview with U.S. Department of Defense official, Manila, March 2005.

Singapore, the security forces do not have at their disposal special arrest, detention, and surveillance powers that can be used for preemptive purposes.[70] Moreover, as noted above, a fundamental component of the current peace process with the MILF is the provision that MILF's camps remain off-limits to ongoing military operations taking place in Mindanao[71]—a stipulation that has helped to isolate these bases both from wider monitoring and, more importantly, surprise army raids.[72]

Key Judgments

This case study revealed a number of interesting findings both with regard to widening our understanding of terrorism, as well as revealing potential terrorist vulnerabilities. First, in terrorists' cost-benefit analyses for technology exchanges, they appear to weigh *operational benefits* as much as ideology. We expected that religious ideology would underpin JI's rationale for exchanging technologies with Islamist militants in Mindanao. Yet, we found that JI also gained something that would improve its overall operational capabilities: access to safe havens in the southern Philippines that it would otherwise not have in Indonesia.

---

[70] A far-reaching Internal Security Act (ISA) is in place in both Singapore and Malaysia, which has had the effect of greatly expanding the search, arrest, surveillance and seizure powers of the security forces as well as allowing for preemptive arrests on the grounds of suspicion or mere association with the aims of terrorism. Such laws would not be countenanced in the Philippines where there is an active reticence on the part of wider civil society to sanction the institution of special or emergency legislation on account of the abuses that occurred under the Marcos dictatorship.

[71] These operations essentially take place under the auspices of the joint U.S.-Filipino Balikitan Exercises (first initiated in 2002 and then reenacted in 2004) and are currently directed at flushing out residual ASG strongholds in Jolo and Zamboanga. See ICG (2004, p. 7); "DND: Mindanao War Games to Target Jema'ah Agents," *ABS-CBN News*, June 28, 2004; Davis (2003, p. 17); "Back to the Jungle," *The Economist*, March 1, 2003; "When Local Anger Joins Global Hate," *The Economist*, October 19, 2002; and "Grumblings Surface During 'Balikitan,'" *The Philippine Daily Inquirer*, February 3, 2002.

[72] Personal interviews with security analysts, Western diplomats, and intelligence officials, Honolulu, Manila, and Singapore, March–April 2005.

Second, terrorists' desire for *credibility* in their local support community also seems to affect the cost-benefit analysis for technology exchanges. Filipino militants apparently believed that their association with JI would provide them with greater credibility with radical Muslim populations in the southern Philippines, and perhaps the global Salafi Jihadi movement as well. It is arguable that this factor, in addition to increasing operational capabilities, was instrumental in influencing Filipino militants' decision to exchange technologies with JI.

Third, terrorist groups may be able to improve their capabilities significantly by exchanging technology and knowledge. Our research suggests that new technologies, many built on preexisting knowledge (for example, IEDs detonated remotely by cell phone rather than by a timing device), allowed militants both to reduce the number of faulty detonations and to increase the number of deaths per attack.

Fourth, in the case of militants in the southern Philippines, successful exchanges appeared to be the result of (1) trust built on a similar ideological worldview and (2) cognizance that the cease-fire between the MILF and Manila reduced the risk that counterterrorism officials might capture valuable technologies, JI trainers, or newly taught Filipino militants. Conceivably, the safe havens in Mindanao also allowed more opportunity for direct person-to-person contact, increasing the probability for successful exchanges.

Although there is good reason to believe that each of these factors facilitated the exchange of technology in Mindanao, they also represent potential vulnerabilities. Chapter Six explores how the U.S. government might develop policies to exploit these weaknesses.

Combined, these factors appear to have provided a significant point of reference for JI and Filipino Islamist weapon technology cooperation. The available evidence suggests that the influence of these exchanges has been profound and may, indeed, be one of the more important variables that is currently impacting on the nature, scope, and attendant threat potential of regional Muslim extremism. It is in this context that Joseph Mussomeli, the U.S. Embassy chargé d'affaires in Manila, has described Mindanao as the "new Mecca for transnational terrorism" in Southeast Asia.[73]

---

[73] Ulph (2005b).

CHAPTER FOUR

West Bank and Gaza:
Israel as the Common Enemy

In May 2000, Israeli military forces withdrew from southern Lebanon after almost 18 years of occupation. Hizballah declared victory. Approximately five months later, the al-Aqsa Intifada—the second Palestinian·"uprising"—broke out in the West Bank and Gaza Strip (WBGS). Although the causes of the al-Aqsa Intifada are complex and varied, it is clear that many Palestinian militants took heart from Hizballah's successful campaign against Israel.[1] Indeed, Marwan Barghouti, a key leader of the al-Aqsa Intifada until his arrest in April 2002, stated the following:

> To be candid, I must say that Israel's withdrawal from Lebanon was indeed one contributing factor to the [al-Aqsa] Intifada. I won't say that it was the single reason, but the Palestinians looked on carefully as the army pulled out of Lebanon. They asked how could it be that Israel was able to withdraw from an entanglement of nearly 20 years—all in one night. Not one soldier remained behind. So I say that if that was accomplished literally overnight

[1]   A number of factors contributed to the Israeli government's decision to withdraw from southern Lebanon. Fundamentally, Israel occupied this area to create a buffer zone from attacks by Palestinian militants. Hizballah did not emerge until after the Israeli occupation. From 1982 to 2000, however, Hizballah continued to kill and kidnap Israeli soldiers to the extent that the Israeli public came to believe that the "buffer zone" was ineffective and the cost of occupation too high. Thus, the perception that the Israeli military withdrew from southern Lebanon as a result of Hizballah's guerrilla campaign is reasonable. In fact, the Israeli military made a determined effort not to "flee" the Gaza Strip in the same way, by refusing to withdraw under fire and demolishing the Palestinian militants' leadership before it left.

in Lebanon, the retreat from Ramallah to Tel-Aviv should require no more than three nights at most.[2]

Despite this, and the fact that experts agree that Hizballah has aided Palestinian militants in the past, very little attention has been given to the questions of how and to what extent Hizballah helped Palestinian militants in the al-Aqsa Intifada. This situation began to change in January 2002, after Israeli security forces interdicted a maritime smuggling vessel, referred to as *Karine A*, on its way to the Gaza Strip. The *Karine A* contained approximately 50 tons of weapons and explosives. Among the weapons were *katyusha*[3] rockets, hitherto unknown in WBGS, but among the most effective weapons in the Hizballah arsenal. With *katyusha* rockets, Palestinian militants still could not have threatened Tel Aviv from Gaza, which is approximately 70 kilometers away. But *katyusha* rockets could reach a number of Israeli cities from the West Bank, including Jerusalem. *Karine A* made it clear that Hizballah had decided to take a more active role than most people had realized in the Palestinians' fight against Israel.

This chapter explores exchanges between Hizballah and the Palestinian militant groups during the al-Aqsa Intifada. It also delineates what factors led to effective exchanges and what factors hindered the success of these exchanges.

Background: Militant Groups in the West Bank and Gaza Strip

We examined four different militant groups in this study of technology and knowledge exchanges in WBGS. These groups are Lebanese Hizballah, al-Aqsa Martyrs Brigades, Hamas, and Palestinian Islamic Jihad (PIJ). The following section provides a brief background for each of these militant groups.

---

[2] "Hizballah Lends Its Services to the Palestinian Intifada," *Jane's Intelligence Review,* November 1, 2001.

[3] *Katyusha* rockets are Soviet-era, 107-mm or 122-mm caliber, with a range of approximately 15 to 20 kilometers.

Hizballah

In the 1970s and early 1980s, the Palestinian Liberation Organization (PLO) used southern Lebanon as a base of operations for its attacks against Israel. To reduce these attacks, the Israel Defense Forces (IDF) invaded and occupied southern Lebanon in June 1982. The purpose of "Operation Peace for the Galilee" was to devastate the political and military leadership of the PLO as well as to deny militants easy access to Israel.[4] This operation—and subsequent occupation—was successful, in part. Palestinian militants evacuated Lebanon in August 1982, under the watchful eyes of a Multinational Force,[5] and dispersed to a number of training camps throughout the Muslim world. The PLO's political leaders also left Beirut at that time, relocating to Algiers.[6]

But a new threat emerged in southern Lebanon in the early 1980s: the indigenous Shi'ite militant group known as Hizballah or "Party of God." A cluster of independent militias originally merged to form Hizballah. Led by Abbas al-Musawi until 1992, Hizballah initially received training from Iran's Revolutionary Guards in southern Lebanon.[7] Its overarching objective was to remove the presence of Western military forces—including the Multinational Forces and the IDF—from southern Lebanon. To do this, Hizballah attacked Israeli military targets as well as the Multinational Forces; it also kidnapped Western journalists, embassy officials, and professors at the American University of Beirut. The following lists some of these early attacks:[8]

---

[4] For more information on Israeli operations in southern Lebanon, see Ian Black and Benny Morris, *Israel's Secret Wars*, New York: Grove Weidenfeld, 1991.

[5] This Multinational Force includes U.S., French, and Italian soldiers.

[6] For more history on the PLO, see Helena Cobban, *The Palestinian Liberation Organization: People, Power, and Politics*, Cambridge: Cambridge University Press, 1984.

[7] Amal Saad-Ghorayeb, *Hizbu'llah: Politics and Religion*, London: Pluto Press, 2002, pp. 14–15. See also "Baalbek Seen as Staging Area for Terrorism," *The Washington Post*, January 9, 1984; and Carl Anthony Wege, "Hizbollah Organization," *Studies in Conflict and Terrorism*, Vol. 17, No. 2, 1994, pp. 151–164.

[8] For more information on these and other attacks in this study, see the MIPT Terrorism Knowledge Base (which integrates data from the RAND Terrorism Chronology and RAND-MIPT Terrorism Incident Database, the Terrorism Indictment database, and DFI International's research on terrorist organizations) (Memorial Institute for the Prevention

- In March 1983, Hizballah members drove a truck loaded with explosives next to an IDF convoy; the detonation killed or injured all 120 members of the convoy.
- In October 1983, Hizballah members crashed trucks packed with explosives into the barracks of U.S. and French multinational peacekeepers, killing a total of 299 individuals and injuring an additional 75.
- In March 1984, Hizballah members abducted CNN Beirut bureau chief Jeremy Levin. He eventually escaped.
- In December 1984, Hizballah members hijacked a Kuwait Airlines flight on its way from Kuwait to Pakistan, diverting it to Tehran. The hijackers killed two U.S. Agency for International Development passengers, but Iranian security officials rescued the remaining hostages.
- In June 1985, three Hizballah members hijacked a TWA flight en route from Athens to Rome, diverting it to Lebanon. They eventually released all of the hostages, apparently in exchange for the release of some Shiite prisoners by Israel.
- On September 26, 1985, Hizballah members kidnapped two British women: One taught at the American University of Beirut and the other managed a restaurant. They were released 13 days later.

In the 1980s, Hizballah and its competitor, Amal, as well as Christian militias, began a series of attacks and counterattacks that threw Lebanon into civil war.[9] Part of the backdrop for these attacks was a rivalry between Syria and Iran for control over militants in Lebanon. The result was a compromise, enforced by Syrian security forces: Hizballah could keep its weapons, but it should focus its attention on

---

of Terrorism, *MIPT Terrorism Knowledge Base*, undated). See also Kim Cragin, "Hizballah, the Party of God," in Brian A. Jackson, John C. Baker, Peter Chalk, Kim Cragin, John V. Parachini, and Horacio R. Trujillo, *Aptitude for Destruction*, Vol. 2: *Case Studies of Organizational Learning in Five Terrorist Groups*, Santa Monica, Calif.: RAND Corporation, MG-332-NIJ, 2005, pp. 37–55; and Frontline, "Terrorist Attacks on Americans, 1979–1988: The Attacks, the Groups, and the U.S. Response," *Target America*, October 4, 2001

[9] For more information on the civil war on Lebanon, see Robert Fisk, *Pity the Nation: Lebanon at War*, Oxford: Oxford University Press, 2001.

removing the Israeli military from southern Lebanon rather than on Western targets in Lebanon or elsewhere.[10] This shift in focus also dovetailed ideologically with Hizballah, which views the liberation of Jerusalem from Israel as a key pan-Islamic jihad.[11]

Israel withdrew from southern Lebanon in May 2000. Prior to this withdrawal, Hizballah and the IDF engaged in series of escalations and counterescalations, all in a bid to gain control over southern Lebanon. For example, Israel attempted to reduce popular support for Hizballah by demolishing houses and villages linked to the group. Hizballah responded by creating the Campaign for Reconstruction Institution, which rebuilt homes immediately after IDF destroyed them.[12] Hizballah repaired approximately 1,000 homes between 1988 and 1992.[13] Alternatively, the Israeli government also attempted to remove key Hizballah leaders from the organization. In February 1992, for example, Israeli security forces assassinated Abbas al-Musawi.[14] Similarly, in June 1994, the Israeli Air Force attacked a Hizballah headquarters in Ein Dardara.[15] Hizballah responded to these attacks against its leadership with two suicide bombings against Jewish targets overseas: the March 1992 attack against the Israeli embassy and the July 1994 attack against the Jewish Cultural Center, both in Buenos Aires. This retaliation appears to have deterred any future attacks by IDF against key Hizballah leaders.

On a tactical level, Hizballah also began to improve its capabilities. For example, in the early 1990s, Hizballah introduced IEDs into

---

[10] The civil war in Lebanon ended in approximately 1989. For more information on Hizballah's attacks against Western targets and the deal between Syria and Iran, see Magnus Ranstorp, *Hizb'allah in Lebanon: The Politics of the Western Hostage Crisis*, London: MacMillan Press, 1997.

[11] Saad-Ghorayeb (2002, pp. 75–76); Ranstorp (1997, pp. 49–58).

[12] "Focus on Hizballah," *The Lebanon Report*, Vol. 4, No. 3, 1993, pp. 6–7.

[13] Magnus Ranstorp, "The Strategy and Tactics of Hizballah's Current 'Lebanonization Process,'" *Mediterranean Politics*, Vol. 3, No. 1, Summer 1998, p. 106.

[14] Peter Hirshberg, "Getting Smart," *Jerusalem Post*, December 17, 1992.

[15] "Special Survey: Bombing of the AMIA Building in Buenos Aires," Israeli Ministry of Foreign Affairs, July 19, 1994.

its arsenal for use against Israeli forces.[16] Around that same time, Hizballah also improved the aim and range of its *katyusha* rockets[17] to the extent that it brokered an agreement with IDF: Hizballah would not shoot rockets into the Galilee and IDF would not bomb Hizballah villages in south Lebanon.[18]

These improvements and adaptations continued through the late 1990s until today. For example, Hizballah allegedly began to incorporate night-vision goggles into its arsenal around 1998. By the time of the al-Aqsa Intifada, Hizballah had also begun to experiment with unmanned aerial vehicles (UAVs).[19] Perhaps even more interesting, in November 2004, Hizballah successfully flew a UAV from southern Lebanon over Israel—approximately five minutes—and back toward Lebanon, before it crashed into the sea.[20] Hizballah launched a similar UAV flight in April 2005. These UAV flights indicate that Hizballah has continued to innovate, despite its main adversary's withdrawal from Lebanon.

Hizballah's ability to adapt to IDF countermeasures and improve its overall capabilities contributed to the aforementioned Israeli military withdrawal in May 2000. Since that time, Hizballah increasingly has become involved in the Palestinian struggle against Israel. In Chapter Five, we address the extent to which and how Hizballah's involvement has played itself out in WBGS.

---

[16] "Hizballah Wages Electronic War in South Lebanon," *Jane's Intelligence Review*, February 1, 1995.

[17] Some Israeli experts contend that Iran (allegedly in 2002) transferred longer-range weapons to Hizballah: Fadjr-3 or Fadjr-5 rockets that have a range of 40 to 80 kilometers and could reach Haifa from southern Lebanon (personal interviews, Israel, February 2003). See also Roger Davies, "Small Artillery Rockets Extend Range of Terrorist Attacks on Urban Centers," *Jane's Intelligence Review*, March 1, 2002.

[18] Ehud Barak articulated this agreement in September 1993 ("What Security for the South? Syrian Displeasure Limits Army's Deployment," *The Lebanon Report*, Vol. 4, No. 9, September 1993, p. 5).

[19] Personal interviews with security officials, Israel, June 2005.

[20] Personal interviews with Israeli security officials, Washington, D.C., June 2005. See also "Mohajer (UAV)," *GlobalSecurity.org*, undated Web page.

Al-Aqsa Martyrs Brigades

The Palestinian militant group al-Aqsa Martyrs Brigades has been a recipient of Hizballah's improved technology and knowledge. Until the 1993 Oslo Accords, the PLO was an umbrella organization for a number of different political and military factions that fought for an independent Palestine. Fatah (a reverse acronym for *Harakat al-Tahir al-Filastiniyya*) was one member of the PLO, but eventually came to dominate it by the late 1960s.[21] After Yasser Arafat, the leader of Fatah and the PLO, negotiated the terms of a peace agreement with the Israeli government in the early 1990s, most Fatah members became part of the Palestinian Authority (PA). For example, Fatah members joined the newly formed Palestinian security forces, under the auspices of the PA. They also ran for parliament and became enmeshed in the Palestinian civil bureaucracy. Thus, with the emergence of the al-Aqsa Intifada, it was difficult for Fatah to participate officially in the fight against Israel. The al-Aqsa Martyrs Brigades, therefore, apparently was formed to take on this more militant role. Importantly, at the time of this writing, neither Fatah nor Arafat (until his death in 2004) had recognized the al-Aqsa Martyrs Brigades.

The al-Aqsa Martyrs Brigades has struggled to compete with other militant groups in WBGS for both legitimacy and recruits. To do this, the Brigades must prove that it can challenge the Israeli security forces successfully. This requirement has served to push the Brigades toward the adoption of new technology and tactics. The following lists some attacks by the al-Aqsa Martyrs Brigades since October 2000:

- In January 2002, members of the al-Aqsa Martyrs Brigades opened fire on a bat mitzvah party in Hadera, killing six and wounding 35.
- In March 2002, a member of the al-Aqsa Martyrs Brigades conducted a suicide bombing in Jerusalem's Ultra-Orthodox neighborhood, Me'a Sha'arim, killing nine and wounding 45.

---

[21] Cobban (1984, pp. 10–18).

- In November 2002, members of the al-Aqsa Martyrs Brigades attacked a Likud Party headquarters in Beit She'an, killing six and wounding 43.
- In July 2003, members of the al-Aqsa Martyrs Brigades in Gaza fired mortar shells on a settlement, injuring no one.
- In January 2004, a member of the al-Aqsa Martyrs Brigades conducted a suicide bombing on a bus in Jerusalem, killing eight and wounding approximately 60 individuals.
- In September 2004, members of the al-Aqsa Martyrs Brigades fired two mortars on a settlement in Gaza, injuring no one.
- In January 2005, al-Aqsa Martyrs Brigades and Hamas both claimed responsibility for a suicide truck bombing at the Karni Crossing between Israel and the Gaza Strip. The attacked killed six and wounded 15.[22]

The al-Aqsa Martyrs Brigades is based primarily in the West Bank, where it, reportedly, is organized into military units. These units include the Usama Turkeman Unit, Fadi and Amjad Unit, the Malja Alamariya Unit, and the Nur Yassin Unit.[23] The Brigades also has a smaller presence in Gaza, including the Ayman Jouda and Khan Yunis Units.[24] Israeli security forces assassinated Raed al-Karmi, the leader of al-Aqsa Martyrs Brigades, on January 14, 2002. His successor, Nasser Awais, was arrested in April 2002. Mahmoud Titi, the chief operations officer, subsequently took over the Brigades only to be assassinated by Israeli security forces one month later.[25] These assassinations are why many experts view the Brigades as fragmented and in chaos. They also

---

[22] For more information on these attacks and others in this study, see the MIPT Terrorism Knowledge Base (Memorial Institute for the Prevention of Terrorism, undated).

[23] Intelligence and Terrorism Information Center at the Center for Special Studies, "The 'Al Aqsa Martyrs Brigades' and the Fatah Organization Are One and the Same, and Yasser Arafat Is Their Leader and Commander," April 10, 2005.

[24] "Al-Aqsa Unit Says Israeli Troops Held, Not Killed," Reuters, July 30, 2004.

[25] For more information, see Suzanne Goldenberg, "Israeli Tank Blows up Leading Militant," *The Guardian Unlimited*, May 23, 2002.

may explain why this group has been willing to accept increased support from Hizballah.

Harakat Al-Muqawama Al-Islamiya (Hamas)

Harakat Al-Muqawama Al-Islamiya ("Islamic Resistance Movement") is a Palestinian militant group with cells throughout WBGS. This group also has benefited from Hizballah's technological development and knowledge.

Hamas emerged out of the first Intifada that took place from 1987 until approximately 1992. Hamas' stated goal is the establishment of an Islamic Palestinian state.[26] Hamas militant activities are directed primarily against Israel, in the hopes of forcing Israeli withdrawal from WBGS. In this context, Hamas is viewed as a terrorist organization by Israeli and international audiences alike. But Hamas' activities also are directed toward secular Palestinians, in the hopes of ensuring an Islamic system of government in WBGS. Thus, Hamas is, in many ways, an opponent—or at the very least a competitor—of Fatah and the al-Aqsa Martyrs Brigades.

Ra'id Zakarna conducted one of Hamas' first suicide bombings against a bus near Afula in April 1994.[27] The attack killed eight and wounded an additional 44. Hamas leaders have claimed that the attack was in retaliation for the 1993 Hebron massacre, in which 29 Muslims were shot by an Israeli settler while praying at a local mosque.[28] Since that time, Hamas has been known for its suicide attacks against Israeli civilian targets. The following lists some of these attacks:

---

[26] M. Maqdsi, trans., "The Charter of the Islamic Resistance Movement (Hamas) of Palestine," *Journal of Palestine Studies,* Vol. 22, No. 4, Summer 1993, pp. 122–134.

[27] According to the Institute for Counter-Terrorism in Herzliya, Israel, Hamas conducted its first suicide attack in April 1993. For this attack, a militant drove a van filled with explosives between two parked buses. The buses had earlier been full of IDF soldiers but were empty at the time of detonation.

[28] See "Hamas: Waiting for Secular Nationalism to Self-Destruct— An Interview with Mahmud Zahhar," *Journal of Palestine Studies*, Vol. 24, No. 3, Spring 1995, pp. 81–88; and P. Hilder, "The Nail in the Wood: An Interview with Ismail Abu Shanab," *Open Democracy Ltd.*, 2004.

- In October 1994, Salah Abdel Rahim Suwey detonated an explosive belt on a bus in downtown Tel Aviv, killing 23 and injuring 45. A Hamas member read a printed statement in a Gaza mosque claiming this attack was in retaliation for the assassinations of Hamas members.
- In February 1996, an unknown suicide bomber detonated an explosive belt in the midst of soldiers in Ashqelon, killing three and wounding 25. A Hamas statement read at a Gaza mosque claimed that the attack was in retaliation for the assassination of Yahya Ayyah (the "engineer").
- In May 2001, Mahmoud Ahmed Marmash detonated an explosive belt at HaSharon Shopping Mall in Netanya, killing seven and wounding 50. Sheikh Yasin claimed the attack at a rally in Gaza, stating it was in retaliation for the killing of five Palestinians by Israeli police earlier that month.
- In December 2001, two unknown bombers detonated explosive belts simultaneously in Jerusalem's Ben Yehuda Square; a third car bomb also detonated after emergency responders arrived at the scene, killing 12 and wounding 180. Hamas claimed the attack in a call to al-Manar, Hizballah's television station.
- In March 2002, Shadi Tobassi detonated an explosive belt in a restaurant in Haifa, killing 16 and wounding 46. Hamas claimed the attack in a call to the Abu Dhabi television station, stating that the attacks would continue until Israel pulled its troops out of Ramallah.
- In June 2003, Abdel Muati Shaban detonated an explosive belt on a bus in Jerusalem, killing 18 and wounding 93. He was dressed as a Haredi Jew. In Hebron, masked Hamas gunmen took over a local TV station and ordered the announcer to read a note in which they claimed the attack was retaliation for an assassination attempt against Rantisi (Hamas political spokesperson and leader).

Like the al-Aqsa Martyrs Brigades, Hamas has had to deal with the arrest and assassination of many of its leaders by Israeli security forces. These losses include (1) Yahya Ayyash, Hamas' primary engineer, in January 1996; (2) Saleh Shedhadeh, the leader of Hamas' militant wing, in July 2002; (3) Ismail abu Shanab, Hamas' deputy leader, in August 2003; and (4) Sheikh Yasin, Hamas' founder and leader, in March 2004. But, unlike the al-Aqsa Martyrs Brigades, Hamas apparently has established a succession plan, or at least it has replaced these losses relatively quickly. This quickness may explain, in part, why Hamas has turned to Hizballah less than the Brigades.

Palestinian Islamic Jihad (PIJ)

Finally, the Palestinian Islamic Jihad (PIJ) is another group that has benefited from Hizballah's technological capabilities and knowledge. Fathi al-Shikaki and Abd al-Aziz Auda founded PIJ around 1980.[29] Compared with the other groups in the study, PIJ has remained relatively small with several dozen to perhaps 100 members. PIJ also does not retain an expansive local support network through charitable activities, as do Hamas in WBGS and Hizballah in Lebanon.

The following lists some past PIJ attacks in Israel:

- In December 1993, PIJ members shot an Israeli soldier near Holon Junction.[30]
- In January 1995, Hamas and PIJ members conducted a suicide bombing at a military bus stop near Netanya, killing 19 and wounding 69.[31]
- In October 2003, PIJ members conducted a suicide bombing at a restaurant in Haifa, killing 21 individuals.

Philosophically, PIJ is a Sunni Muslim militant group whose members do not believe that a revolution can occur from the grassroots (as does Hamas) but rather that it should be forced downward from the political leadership. This philosophy explains, in part, PIJ's reluctance to become involved in social and charitable programs. In this

---

[29] Ziad Abu-Amr, *Islamic Fundamentalism in the West Bank and Gaza*, Bloomington: Indiana University Press, 1994, pp. 93–95.

[30] See "Palestinian Islamic Jihad," *Jane's Terrorism and Insurgency Centre*, undated.

[31] See Australian Government, "Australian National Security," undated Web page.

context, PIJ leaders were influenced by the 1979 Iranian Revolution. Indeed, after Israeli security services deported al-Shikaki in 1988, he apparently made contact with Hizballah and members of the Iranian Revolutionary Guards in southern Lebanon. Many analysts, therefore, argue that PIJ has the closest ties to Hizballah, relative to the other Palestinian groups discussed in this chapter.[32] Israel security services assassinated al-Shikaki in October 1995. Since that time, PIJ's influence in WBGS has diminished.

Rationalizing the Exchange of Technology and Knowledge

Importantly, Hizballah and Palestinian militants have different ideological worldviews. Hizballah is a Shiite organization: Its leaders believe that Ayatollah Khomeini was the divinely inspired ruler of the *ummah*[33] and Hizballah still turns to Iran for spiritual guidance.[34] Most members of the Palestinian militant groups are Sunni, who typically view Shiites as heretical. Moreover, Hizballah and the Palestinian militant groups are all nationalistic—Hizballah with regard to Lebanon and the others with regard to a Palestinian state—and weight these practical concerns above pan-Islamic philosophy[35].

Having said that, Hizballah and the Palestinian militants have a common enemy: Israel. Additionally, Hizballah's leaders repeatedly emphasize their support for the Palestinian cause.[36] And this support is not simply rhetorical. For example, Hizballah fired *katyusha* rockets into northern Israel following the assassination of Hamas leader

---

[32] Personal interview with terrorism expert and author, Jerusalem, June 2005.

[33] Muslim community.

[34] Saad-Ghorayeb (2002, pp. 64–65).

[35] In using the term *pan-Islamic*, we refer to the concept that national boundaries in the Muslim world are not significant. Individuals adhering to this worldview believe that the entire "ummah," or Muslim community, should be governed by one overarching religious authority, similar to the Caliphate.

[36] Saad-Ghorayeb (2002, pp. 75–76).

Sheikh Yasin in 2004.[37] In fact, Hizballah has continued its support for the Palestinian cause despite a decline in empathy within its own support community in Lebanon.[38] This support is, therefore, somewhat surprising, though it may indicate that Hizballah weights its enmity with Israel heavily or its philosophical support for the Palestinian cause sufficiently strong that these factors outweigh the potential for a backlash in southern Lebanon.

From the viewpoint of Palestinian militants, these groups, particularly Hamas, have been reluctant to become too involved with Hizballah in the past to avoid becoming beholden. Yet, at the same time, Palestinian militants experienced significant pressure from Israeli security forces from October 2000 to June 2004. Simply put, during the al-Aqsa Intifada, Palestinian militants needed all the help they could get.

Identifying Exchanges in the West Bank and Gaza

One key difference between this case study and the others in this monograph—including both Mindanao and southwest Colombia—is the pressure exerted by counterterrorism officials on the militant groups.[39] Hamas, PIJ, and the al-Aqsa Martyrs Brigades had to survive intense Israeli counterterrorism and counterinsurgency operations. In response, Palestinian militant groups innovated. To do this, the groups collaborated among themselves, but they also received external support. This support came in the form of money, ammunition and weapon exchanges, and remote instruction, as well as direct person-to-person contact.

---

[37] Adam Shatz, "In Search of Hezbollah-II," *The New York Review of Books*, Vol. 51, No. 8, May 13, 2004.

[38] Personal interviews with terrorism expert and author, Beirut, June 2005.

[39] This trend is similar to what PIRA went through in the 1980s and early 1990s in Northern Ireland. The situation in Northern Ireland today, however, does not require intensive counterterrorism activities.

Another key difference is that the technology exchanges were actually technology transfers: Hizballah provided technology and know-how to the Palestinians and did not receive training in return. Notably, Israeli officials believe that the bulk of Hizballah's aid during the al-Aqsa Intifada has gone to the Brigades. This belief is based on the observation that Israeli counterterrorism efforts fractured the Brigades to the extent that this group needed help more than the others.[40] Having said that, it is clear that all the militant groups in this case study received some degree of technology and knowledge transfer from Hizballah.

Three general patterns exist in technology exchanges between Hizballah and Palestinian militants. First, Hizballah has attempted to provide direct person-to-person instruction to different Palestinian cells. Second, Hizballah has engaged in physical technology transfers to Palestinian militants. Third, Hizballah may be attempting to move beyond exchanges and take some operational control over al-Aqsa Martyrs Brigades. The following sections address these general patterns in more detail.

Direct Person-to-Person Instruction

Hizballah has attempted to provide direct person-to-person instruction as well as weapons to local militant groups in WBGS. For example, in March 2004, Israel's Ministry of Foreign Affairs issued a press release on the arrest of Shadi Abu Alhatzin, the leader of the aforementioned Khan Yunis cell in the Gaza Strip.[41] Alhatzin's father was Palestinian, but his mother was Lebanese. He apparently came into contact with Hizballah in 2000 through his mother's family. Although Alhatzin himself communicated with Hizballah remotely, two associates—Bassam Abu Nimr and Ismail Garabeli (arrested in 2002)—allegedly traveled to Lebanon for basic weapons and guerrilla warfare training.[42] This example illustrates an effort on the part of Palestinian

---

[40] See "Al-Aqsa Martyrs Brigades," earlier in this chapter.

[41] "ISA Arrests Head of Gaza Strip Hezbollah Cell," Israel Ministry of Foreign Affairs, March 10, 2004.

[42] "ISA Arrests Head of Gaza Strip Hezbollah Cell" (2004).

militants to improve their technology or the efficiency of existing technologies by interacting with Hizballah trainers in southern Lebanon. Notably, Israeli officials believe that these transfers have been successful, adding that Hizballah has invited the best Palestinian fighters to southern Lebanon, thereby ensuring greater efficiency.[43]

Alhatzin also revealed that, in 2003, a Hizballah representative came to Khan Yunis to provide training in communication security.[44] Operational security has been a key problem for Palestinian militants in the al-Aqsa Intifada, and Israeli human intelligence and electronic surveillance capabilities are feared and respected by many Palestinians.[45] It is, therefore, logical that local militant cells would request help in communication security. Similarly, interviews with Israeli security officials suggest that Qeis Ubeid, an Israeli Arab from Taibeh associated with Hizballah, aided the al-Aqsa Martyrs Brigades cell in Nablus. This aid came in the form of target selection and recruitment. Ubeid apparently also facilitated local militants' access to Hizballah training camps in southern Lebanon.[46]

In a November 2004 article in the Israeli newspaper, *Ha'aretz*, journalist Amos Harel observed that Hizballah had stopped attempting to send explosives experts and other trainers into WBGS. Hizballah had shifted its approach to rely on couriers to exchange this knowledge instead.[47] This shift was likely a response to increases in counterterrorism pressure from Israel: At a certain threshold of arrests, Hizballah may have decided that the risk of direct person-to-person contact was too high.

---

[43] Personal interview with counterterrorism expert, Israel, June 2005.

[44] "ISA Arrests Head of Gaza Strip Hezbollah Cell" (2004).

[45] Personal interview with journalist, Jerusalem, August 2004. See, for example, Ghazi Hamid, "Electronic Occupation," *Palestine Report*, June 22, 2005.

[46] Personal interviews with Israeli security officials, Washington, D.C., June 2005. See also "Assessing Hizballah's West Bank Foothold," *PeaceWatch #463: Special Forum Report*, June 18, 2004.

[47] Amos Harel, "Hezbollah's Terror Factory in the PA," *Ha'aretz*, November 1, 2004.

Physical Technology Exchanges

Hizballah also has provided Palestinian militants with physical technologies as well as relevant instructions for their use. For example, in January 2002, Israeli security forces intercepted the aforementioned *Karine A*. Israeli authorities believe that the weapons on this vessel came from Hizballah and Iran.[48] Items in this shipment included the following:

- ***Katyusha* rockets (122 mm and 107 mm).** These rockets can be launched from the back of a truck or from the ground. They have a range of 15 to 20 kilometers (12.5 miles).
- **AT-3 Sagger missiles.** These weapons, likely produced by Iran, are portable, wire-guided, antitank missiles. They have a range of approximately 0.5 to 3.0 kilometers.[49]
- **YM-III Iranian antitank mines.** The YM-III is a plastic-cased, minimum-metal, antitank blast mine. The explosive weight is approximately 5.7 kg and the operating force is approximately 450–900 kg.[50]

Notably, at the time of this writing, Palestinians had not yet used *katyusha* rockets, Sagger missiles, or YM-III antitank mines against Israel. Our research also did not find any evidence that these weapons had been used since that time, indicating that the interdiction of *Karine A*

---

[48] "Seizing of the Palestinian Weapons Ship *Karine A*," Israel Ministry of Foreign Affairs, January 4, 2002.

[49] Hizballah apparently used Sagger missiles against Israeli forces in southern Lebanon until early 1999. At this point, Hizballah managed to upgrade its capabilities—likely with the help of Iran or Syria—and obtain BGM-71 TOW missiles (tube-launched, optically tracked, and wire guided), which in general have a longer range and are more powerful. See Leslie Susser, "Hizballah Masters the TOW," *The Jerusalem Report*, March 13, 2000; and "The Secrets Behind Hezbollah's Recent Military Successes," *Middle East Intelligence Bulletin*, Vol. 2, No. 3, March 2000.

[50] The weapons listed here were not the only ones on the *Karine A,* but they are the most sophisticated. They also are the only ones not previously used by Palestinian militants. Other weapons included various mortars, RPG-7s, and RPG-18s. See "YM-III," *Jane's*, April 16, 2003. See also "Seizing of the Palestinian Weapons Ship *Karine A*" (2002).

halted, at least for the time being, the introduction of these technologies into WBGS.

Similarly, in May 2003, Israeli security forces intercepted the *Abu Hasan*, another boat filled with weapons from Hizballah on its way to WBGS.[51] The *Abu Hasan's* cargo included Qassam rockets,[52] as well as a remote-controlled explosive-device system that contained a radio-activation system and 15 electronic delay units.[53] In addition to these technologies, the *Abu Hasan's* cargo contained CD-ROMs with instructions for making various IEDs and for conducting guerrilla warfare.[54] One such explosive device was a bowl-shaped shrapnel explosive charge, which Israeli security forces subsequently discovered in WBGS in June 2005. Shrapnel from this explosive device successfully penetrated an IDF armored vehicle, representing a significant increase in Palestinian militants' operational capabilities.

The CD-ROMs also included information on building different types of suicide belts as well as detonation devices. Suicide bombers adopted these special detonation devices in two different attacks, one that took place in August 2004 and another in January 2005.[55] It is clear, therefore, that although Israeli security forces intercepted the *Abu Hasan* shipment, this knowledge eventually made its way from Hizballah into WBGS. More importantly, Palestinian militants successfully adopted and deployed these weapons against Israeli civilian and military targets.

---

[51] "The Seizing of the *Abu Hasan*," Israel Ministry of Foreign Affairs, May 22, 2003.

[52] Qassam rockets are improvised devices made of steel and filled with explosives. The rockets' length ranges from approximately 3 feet to 7 feet long. The Qassam rockets are not very accurate and have a reach of up to 12 miles. Palestinian militants began to deploy these rockets during the al-Aqsa Intifada in response to Israeli closures, the security fence, and military checkpoints (personal interviews with Israeli security officials, Tel Aviv, June 2005). See, for example, "Qassam Rockets: Crude but Fearsome," *BBC News*, September 29, 2004.

[53] "The Seizing of the *Abu Hasan*" (2003).

[54] "The Seizing of the *Abu Hasan*" (2003). See also Alon Ben-David, "Gaza: The Ghost of Lebanon," *Jane's Defence Weekly*, May 26, 2004.

[55] Personal interviews with terrorism experts and security officials, Tel Aviv and Washington, D.C., June 2005.

Beyond these shipments, other technologies have emerged in WBGS, which Israeli security officials believe originated with Hizballah. For example, Hizballah developed a rock camouflage for IEDs along the Lebanon-Israel border in the 1990s. Israeli officials have stated that a military patrol discovered this type of hidden IED in WBGS in January 2005.[56] Well-camouflaged IEDs present a difficult and unique challenge to military patrols and randomly placed checkpoints. The introduction of this camouflage, therefore, exemplifies another increase in the operational effectiveness of Palestinian militants.

Importantly, these technologies did not have to come into WBGS via maritime trafficking. Evidence exists of a number of different smuggling routes and methods that Hizballah could use to exchange these physical technologies. In March 2004, for example, Israeli police arrested Majad Husam Kna'aneh, a Palestinian associated with Fatah. Majad was smuggling small appliances from Jordan to Jenin in the West Bank; the appliances hid electronic instructions on how to make IEDs.[57] Additionally, Israeli security forces launched Operation Rainbow against smuggling routes from Egypt into Gaza in May 2004. During this operation, Israeli forces discovered and destroyed three tunnels that ran from Rafah[58] underground into the Sinai.[59] Local residents traditionally have used the tunnels to smuggle black-market goods and even workers in and out of Egypt. But the smugglers also

---

[56] Personal interviews with terrorism experts and security officials, Tel Aviv and Washington, D.C., June 2005.

[57] "Two Israeli Arab Brothers Recruited by Hezbollah, Arrested," communicated by the Israeli Prime Minister's Media Adviser, March 5, 2004.

[58] Rafah is situated on the border between Israel and Egypt. It has approximately 130,000 inhabitants.

[59] Doron Almog, "Tunnel-Vision in Gaza," *The Middle East Quarterly*, Vol. 11, No. 3, Summer 2004. Almog states that, between October 2000 and January 2004, Israeli forces discovered and destroyed 94 different smuggling tunnels. The border between Rafah and Egypt is approximately 4 kilometers long and 100 meters wide, also referred to as the "Philadelphi corridor." The tunnels are used to smuggle people, goods, and weapons in and out of the refugee camp.

have benefited from the increasing demand for weapons within WBGS since the start of the al-Aqsa Intifada.[60]

Beyond Technology Exchanges?

Finally, some reports have suggested that Hizballah has attempted to move beyond technology exchanges, taking operational control of some al-Aqsa Martyrs Brigades cells. Israel's Intelligence and Terrorism Information Center, for example, issued a report in January 2005 stating that Hizballah-operated cells in WBGS had conducted 68 attacks in 2004.[61] Some commentators speculate that Hizballah is taking a more active role in WBGS to undermine the ongoing efforts at compromise and peace by Palestinian Authority Chairman Mahmoud Abbas.

Other information contradicts this assessment. In his aforementioned article, Amos Harel stated that Israeli security services identified 51 cells "operated by the Hizballah" in 2004.[62] At the same time, Harel observed that Hizballah did not provide these cells with tactical instructions, but rather pulled them together and then left them alone, adopting a "launch and forget" approach.[63] Harel's observations parallel that of journalist Ehud Ya'ari, writing for *The Jerusalem Report*. In his October 2004 article titled "Unit 1800," Ya'ari noted that Hizballah had designated a special unit to coordinate the militant group's activities in WBGS. Unit 1800, according to Ya'ari, was extending its control in WBGS through the exchange of funds, networking between cells, and importing new technologies. But Hizballah maintained these efforts only by "remote control."[64]

It is too soon to tell whether or not Hizballah is taking over Palestinian militant cells. This takeover would be significant, however, both

---

[60] Almog (2004).

[61] "Iran and Hezbollah as Instigators of Terrorism," *Special Information Bulletin*, report by the Intelligence and Terrorism Information Center in Tel Aviv, January 12, 2005.

[62] Harel (2004).

[63] Harel (2004).

[64] Ehud Ya'ari, "Unit 1800," *The Jerusalem Report*, October 18, 2004.

for Israeli security services and for our understanding of terrorism in general. Hizballah has no interest in a peace process between Israel and the Palestinian Authority; thus, it could use its operational control of these militant cells to undermine the peace process. On a theoretical level, this takeover could be indicative of another rationale for technology exchanges: If a militant group has already won its fight, it may be searching for another "purpose" and is using these exchanges to take on another conflict. Having said that, interviewees in the region acknowledge that Hizballah's presence is becoming increasingly apparent.[65] Yet Hizballah does not appear to be directing al-Aqsa, Hamas, or PIJ cells. Rather, Hizballah provides technology and know-how to help these militant groups achieve their own objectives.

Contextualizing the Exchanges

As previously mentioned, the emergence of the al-Aqsa Intifada played a significant role in the intensity of technology exchanges from Hizballah to Palestinian militants. Palestinian militants and Israeli security forces engaged in an impressive series of attacks and counterattacks over a period of approximately four years (from October 2000 to September 2004). Most experts agree that the violence in Israel and WBGS during that time was the most significant experienced by either side to date. Data substantiate this belief. According to the RAND-MIPT Terrorism Incident Database, approximately 677 Israelis died in terrorist attacks during the al-Aqsa Intifada, as compared with 151 in the first Intifada (1988–1992).[66] The data on Palestinian deaths are somewhat less clear. According to *Palestine Monitor*, a publication by a consortium of Palestinian nongovernmental organizations, 3,334 Palestinians also died from October 2000 to September 2004.[67] But

---

[65] Personal interviews with terrorism experts, Beirut and Jerusalem, June 2005.

[66] Note, these figures only reflect civilian and police casualties in Israel. They do not include military casualties nor Israelis killed within Palestinian-controlled territory.

[67] For more information, see "Palestinian Intifada—4th Anniversary," *Palestine Monitor*, undated.

a report from the Institute for Counter-Terrorism in Herzliya, Israel, states that Israel was responsible for only 568 Palestinian noncombatant deaths as compared with 420 Israeli noncombatant deaths.[68] Either way, this operational tempo dictated that Palestinian militants attempt to overcome new Israeli countermeasures, and Israeli security forces attempt to disrupt new innovations by Palestinian militants. It also explains the wide range of technologies exchanged, from Qassam rockets to rocket-propelled grenades to camouflage for IEDs. In many ways, Hizballah behaved more like a "state sponsor" than a fellow terrorist organization, because it provided Palestinians with both basic supplies and new technologies.

Key Judgments

In the case of Hizballah and the Palestinian militants, Hizballah transferred technology and knowledge to the Palestinians, perhaps gaining credibility and purpose in exchange. A number of important technology and knowledge transfers between Hizballah and Palestinian militants succeeded. They provided Palestinian militants with essential technologies to compete with the IDF in the escalation-counterescalation of the al-Aqsa Intifada. Trust, based on a mutual enmity toward Israel, contributed to this success: During the al-Aqsa Intifada at least, Palestinian militants could rely on Hizballah to protect their interests. Similarly, the technologies that Hizballah transferred most successfully were those that built on existing basic know-how in WBGS, such as IEDs and suicide bombing devices. Hizballah was also able to use existing smuggling routes to transfer weapons and descriptive knowledge to WBGS.

At first glance, Hizballah's behavior contradicts the findings in our Mindanao case study somewhat, with regard to rationale. At first glance, ideology, credibility, and enmity toward Israel appear to have motivated Hizballah more than any direct *operational benefit*, since it

---

[68] Don Radlauer, "The 'al-Aqsa Intifada'—An Engineered Tragedy: Summary of Findings," May 21, 2003.

did not gain any. Hizballah also took on greater risk than JI did in Mindanao, because the Palestinians could not offer its trainers safe havens in WBGS. So one might argue that intangible benefits—such as ideology, credibility, and enmity toward Israel—outweighed practical considerations in Hizballah's calculus for transferring technologies. But this first-glance assessment does not take into account shifts in Hizballah's behavior: Primarily, as IDF began to arrest more and more Hizballah trainers, it reduced direct person-to-person contact in favor of remote physical technology transfers. Thus, although Hizballah did not receive any direct *operational benefit*, it did suffer *operational costs* from the exchanges. The shift in Hizballah's behavior, therefore, suggests that that the intangible benefits that Hizballah's leadership derived from transferring technology did not outweigh the operational costs of losing skilled trainers.

Additionally, we identified two potential barriers to technology exchanges in this case study. The first barrier is a lack of opportunity for direct person-to-person contact. Hizballah expended significant resources to send trainers south to WBGS and Palestinian militants attempted to send trainees to Lebanon. Yet Israeli counterterrorism efforts made travel between WBGS and southern Lebanon much more difficult. These efforts included increased patrols along the Gaza coastline as well as military checkpoints at various locations along key roadways. Because Israeli security forces were able to frustrate Hizballah's efforts at direct contact, therefore, they reduced the aggregate success of technology transfers to WBGS.

Second, turnovers in leadership within Palestinian militant groups, due to Israeli counterterrorism activities, also may have acted as a barrier to successful technology transfers. It is clear that counterterrorism pressure placed significant operational security requirements on the militant groups, as evidenced by concern over communication security by al-Aqsa Martyrs Brigades and Hamas. Thus, it is unlikely that leaders were able to make decisions on what technologies to adopt, for example, in a strategic manner. In the same way, the high turnover of leadership likely impinged on groups' ability to make strategic use of technological resources. We expect that this pressure was responsible for our observation that Palestinian militants—with the exception of

Hamas—for the most part attempted to adopt whatever technology Hizballah would provide, without significant thought for what might be the most effective or efficient use of resources.

CHAPTER FIVE

Southwest Colombia:
A Safe Haven for Mutually Beneficial Exchanges

In August 2001, a month before al Qaeda attacked the World Trade Center and the Pentagon using airplanes as (actively guided) cruise missiles, Colombian authorities arrested three members of the Provisional Irish Republican Army (PIRA) at the airport in Bogotá traveling on false passports. These three men—Niall Connolly, Martin McCauley, and James Monaghan—had just arrived in Bogotá following a five-week tour in the *despeje*, an area of the country that the Colombian government ceded to the Revolutionary Armed Forces of Colombia (FARC) in 1998. A Colombian court indicted Connolly, McCauley, and Monaghan in February 2002 for spending their time in the *despeje* training FARC militants in the use of explosives, including homemade mortars.[1]

---

[1] Adam Ward and James Hackett, eds., "The IRA's Foreign Links: Externalising Its Expertise?" *IISS Strategic Comments*, Vol. 9, No. 5, July 2003. It is important to keep in mind that this is not the first time that FARC and PIRA have allegedly exchanged knowledge and information. PIRA purportedly initiated contact with FARC in 1997 through the ETA, with which PIRA has a long-standing relationship and has exchanged knowledge and technical know-how, particularly in bomb making. According to an April 2002 U.S. Department of State report, one of the three PIRA men, Connolly, Sinn Fein's representative in Cuba, initiated the contact with FARC in 1997; and, from 1998 to 2001, at least 15 PIRA militants have traveled to Colombia, along with Iranian, Cuban, and Basque terrorists, to train FARC. One expert alleged that senior PIRA leaders would have sanctioned this kind of an exchange of technology with another militant group, even though they are publicly adhering to a cease-fire. Notably, PIRA has a long-standing policy prohibiting "freelancing" by its members; as such, the Colombia Three did not likely act alone, despite vehement denials from Sinn Fein, which does not want to be seen as violating the cease-fire. U.S. Secretary of State Colin Powell, responding to the information that this relationship developed after the

Although the "Colombia Three" claimed initially that they were "ecotourists" and later that they were liaising with FARC to understand their peace process, Colombian authorities—in addition to questioning the inconsistency in their explanations—noticed an almost instantaneous improvement in FARC's ability to conduct more sophisticated and lethal operations in Colombia. Beginning in early 2001, FARC began intensifying its operations, killing more than 400 members of the Colombian armed forces in 18 months, using car bombs, "secondary devices,"[2] and homemade mortars. In addition, the group expanded its campaign to Colombian cities, conducting large-scale urban operations, including the February 2003 bombing of the El Nogal country club in Bogotá that killed 36 people.[3]

FARC also displayed an ability to use radio-controlled improvised mortars, a technological capability that only PIRA and ETA had previously demonstrated.[4] Members of the Colombian armed forces subsequently recovered captured barracks-busting mortars believed to be similar to those used by PIRA in Northern Ireland.[5]

The Colombia Three were acquitted in April 2004 after a lengthy trial and released from prison in June but were ordered to stay in the country. A superior court in Colombia overturned the acquittal in December 2004, and the three were sentenced to 17 years in prison. They had already fled the country, however, and are still on the run.[6]

This case study examines the specifics of the exchange of technology and knowledge between FARC and PIRA, first looking at the brief histories of these two groups and commonalities that would make

---

1997 peace process began in Northern Ireland, said on a trip to Bogotá in December 2002 that the groups were "sharing experiences and knowledge."

[2] Secondary devices are a series of bombs detonated after a smaller explosion has killed targets concentrated in one area.

[3] Ward and Hackett (2003).

[4] Ward and Hackett (2003).

[5] John F. Murphy, Jr., "The IRA and the FARC in Colombia," *International Journal of Intelligence and Counterintelligence*, Vol. 18, No. 1, Spring 2005, pp. 76–88 [p. 81].

[6] Jeremy McDermott, "IRA Trio Leave Lethal Legacy in Colombia," *The Scotsman*, January 2, 2005a.

them likely to share technology. Second, we explore the rationale used by each organization for the exchange of technology. Third, we look at how both FARC and PIRA attempted to improve their capabilities through the exchange of technology, and finally put this case study into context with the organizational theory behind why a group would exchange technology and knowledge with another organization.

Background

PIRA and FARC are two very distinct militant groups, but they share some similarities of purpose that have led them to seek each other's help and expertise.

The Provisional Irish Republican Army (PIRA)

PIRA is one of the most sophisticated terrorist groups in the world. The group's campaign in Northern Ireland began in 1969 when the Provisionals split from the Dublin-based Official IRA over differences in strategy, and officially ended in 1997 when the group called a cease-fire, although PIRA splinter groups such as the Real Irish Republican Army (RIRA) and the Continuity Irish Republican Army (CIRA) are still responsible for low-level violence in Northern Ireland. PIRA's membership is primarily drawn from the Roman Catholic population of Northern Ireland, but its fundamental raison d'etre is to force British withdrawal from Northern Ireland and to establish a "United Ireland" where all 32 counties are under the same socialist self-rule.[7] To accomplish this goal, PIRA militants have attacked transportation links and economic targets in Northern Ireland and on the mainland, British Army soldiers and installations in Northern Ireland, police officers and installations of the Royal Ulster Constabulary (RUC),[8] and

---

[7] "Provisional IRA," *Jane's World Insurgency and Terrorism Database*, June 6, 2005.

[8] The RUC was renamed the Police Service of Northern Ireland (PSNI) in 2001 as a result of recommendations made in the Patten Report, which was published by The Independent Commission on Policing in Northern Ireland, established as part of the Good Friday Agreement in April 1998.

other Protestant Loyalists. PIRA also incorporated a Marxist element in their political platform, which argued that the working-class people of Northern Ireland are oppressed under British rule and will only be liberated once self-rule has been established.[9]

PIRA has carried out numerous attacks in Northern Ireland, the Republic of Ireland, and on the British mainland in the last 30 years. The group specialized in remote-controlled and automatically detonated explosive devices, and either pre-positioned these bombs or planted them in vehicles to conduct their attacks.[10] Several of PIRA's more significant attacks include the following:

- In 1972, PIRA planted and exploded 22 bombs, killing nine people and wounding 130 in what was referred to afterward as "Bloody Friday."
- In August 1979, PIRA murdered Earl Mountbatten, cousin of Queen Elizabeth, and three of his associates in County Sligo.
- In October 1984, PIRA detonated a bomb at a hotel in Brighton where Prime Minister Margaret Thatcher and many members of her cabinet were staying. The attack killed Conservative Member of Parliament Sir Anthony Berry as well as four bystanders.
- In 1991, PIRA exploded its first "human bomb" when one of its members drove a vehicle loaded with a 1,000-lb. bomb to a British Army checkpoint in Londonderry, killing six.[11]
- Between 1991 and 1993, PIRA carried out a series of bombings and mortar attacks on the British mainland targeting Heathrow Airport, the Ministry of Defence, train stations, and shopping centers, causing significant disruption to British daily life.
- In February 1996, PIRA ended its cease-fire by conducting three bombing attacks in London: one at Canary Wharf, one target-

---

[9] "Provisional IRA" (2005).

[10] Brian A. Jackson, "Provisional Irish Republican Army," in Jackson et al. (2005b, p. 100).

[11] As compared with most suicide bombers today, the individual responsible for this attack was apparently coerced into participating in a suicide attack.

ing a bus in Aldwych that killed two, and one in a trash can in Fulham.[12]

PIRA officially "decommissioned" its weapon stockpiles in September 2005 and said it was eschewing violence in favor of following a "democratic path."[13] Since PIRA committed to a cease-fire in 1997 and to decommissioning its weapon stockpiles under the 1998 Good Friday Agreement,[14] the group has not conducted any bombing attacks. However, sectarian murders, criminal operations, and low-level violence persist.

The Revolutionary Armed Forces of Colombia (FARC)

FARC was officially established in 1966 as the military wing of the Colombian Communist Party and is the largest, most sophisticated, and most lethal guerrilla group in Colombia. The group has its historical antecedent in the Communist self-defense organizations of the 1940s and 1950s in Colombia, which refused the amnesty offered by the government trying to stop *la Violencia*, the period between 1948 and 1953 when isolated bands of armed guerrillas in rural Colombia fought with conservative landowners to protect their land from being seized.[15] Once order was reestablished by military and then civilian rule in the mid-1950s, these decentralized guerrillas retreated into rural Colombia where they established their own government in an area they called the republic of Marquetalia. Largely ignored until the mid-1960s, Conservative Party politicians saw these guerrillas as a threat and pressured the government to order the Colombian Army

---

[12] "Provisional IRA" (2005).

[13] "IRA Weapons Report Handed Over," *BBC News*, September 26, 2005.

[14] In the Good Friday Accords, PIRA agreed to lay down its arms and peacefully pursue its goal of a united Ireland. To read the Good Friday Agreement in its entirety, see *Good Friday Agreement*, Northern Ireland Office, April 10, 1998.

[15] Marc Chernick, "Appendix: Colombia's Major Guerrilla Movements," in Cynthia J. Arnson, ed., *Comparative Peace Processes in Latin America*, Washington, D.C.: Woodrow Wilson Center Press, 1999, p. 197.

to eradicate them.[16] Manuel Marulanda Velez, also known as *Tiro-fijo* ("Sureshot") helped reorganize the Communist self-defense forces into Fuerzas Armadas Revolucionarios de Colombia (FARC) in 1966, and now heads the group's secretariat.[17] Other leaders include Jorge Briceno, also known as *Mono Jojoy*, the group's chief military commander.[18] FARC's aims are to overthrow the democratic Colombian government and replace it with a Communist regime, as well as to eject U.S. influence from the region.

Despite these stated objectives, some experts argue that, other than establishing rural strongholds and building up their urban base, the group's medium-term political goals are not clear.[19] FARC touts a Marxist ideology that some assert is only aimed at bringing in new recruits, rather than serving as an integral part of the group's policy.[20] Indeed, much of the group's activity in recent years appears focused on gaining control over drug and arms smuggling operations.[21] The area commonly referred to as FARC's *despeje* is situated between two of the largest coca-growing areas in Colombia, and the group's annual drug revenue is assessed to be around $170 million.[22] According to one source, FARC leaders do not live in luxury, however, so it is difficult to assess this group solely as profit seeking.[23]

FARC grew from 350 fighters in 1966 to 15,000–20,000 in 2000 and is organized into seven regional blocs that have from 4 to

---

[16] "Revolutionary Armed Forces of Colombia," Wikipedia, undated(b).

[17] Angel Rabasa and Peter Chalk, *Colombian Labyrinth: The Synergy of Drugs and Insurgency and Its Implications for Regional Stability*, Santa Monica, Calif.: RAND Corporation, MR-1339-AF, 2001, pp. 23–24.

[18] "Revolutionary Armed Forces of Colombia" (undated[b]).

[19] "Fuerzas Armadas Revolucionarias de Colombia (FARC)," *Jane's World Insurgency and Terrorism Database*, January 17, 2005.

[20] "Fuerzas Armadas Revolucionarias de Colombia" (2005).

[21] "Revolutionary Armed Forces of Colombia," Memorial Institute for the Prevention of Terrorism Terrorism Knowledge Base, undated(a).

[22] As of 1999, according to Andres Cala, "Colombia's Cautious Revolutionary," Consortium-news.com, July 25, 1999.

[23] "Fuerzas Armadas Revolucionarias de Colombia" (2005).

20 "fronts" in each bloc. Each front includes columns of up to 100 fighters.[24] FARC militants employ a variety of insurgency and terrorist tactics, including targeting Colombian military and political installations; kidnapping local politicians, foreign military personnel, and business executives; attacking oil pipelines; political extortion of public officials; massacring civilians; and hijacking.[25]

To try to engage FARC in peace talks, former Colombian president Andreas Pastrana authorized the creation of a demilitarized zone in 1998 that ceded five southern districts to FARC. FARC representatives attended peace negotiations the following year, but the group's senior leaders failed to attend, underscoring the weak position of the government.[26] The peace process continued off and on until 2002 when Pastrana ordered the military to regain control of the demilitarized zone after FARC hijacked a domestic flight and kidnapped a senator who was on board. Since peace talks failed, FARC has continued its insurgent campaign, kidnapping three U.S. contractors in February 2003 and attacking civilian and military targets.[27] Beginning in 2001, FARC increased its use of urban terrorism in an attempt to try to regain the operational initiative the Colombian government has maintained, in part due to the $1.3 billion the U.S. government provided Colombia in antidrug assistance starting in 2000.[28] It was at this point that FARC brought in PIRA to help the group prepare for an intensified urban terrorism campaign.[29]

---

[24] Rabasa and Chalk (2001, p. 27).

[25] "Revolutionary Armed Forces of Colombia" (undated[a]).

[26] "Fuerzas Armadas Revolucionarias de Colombia" (2005).

[27] "Revolutionary Armed Forces of Colombia" (undated[a]).

[28] "Summary of Investigation of IRA Links to FARC Narco-Terrorists in Colombia," prepared by the Majority Staff of the House International Relations Committee, Committee on International Relations, U.S. House of Representatives, April 24, 2002.

[29] "Summary of Investigation of IRA Links to FARC Narco-Terrorists in Colombia" (2002).

Similarities of Interest Between PIRA and FARC

FARC and PIRA share a similar worldview. Both profess a nominal Marxist ideology, although it is unclear to what extent they actually believe in their own rhetoric about the subjugation of the working class. Each uses this propaganda, however, to attract new recruits into their respective organizations. Each perceives itself in a weakened role against its respective government, and, as such, this belief may be part of why they agreed to assist each other to help further their campaigns, in much the same way that the British government might assist the Colombian government or vice versa against their respective insurgent threats. Although their guerrilla campaigns are not waged solely on the basis of religion, the fact that they are both rooted in Catholicism may make it easier for these groups to relate to each other's struggle. The FARC/PIRA/ETA relationships may be made easier in part because similar religious convictions help facilitate personal relationships between members of these groups and aid in forming bonds of trust.

Although the majority of terrorist groups, despite their ideological leanings, engage in some criminality, both FARC and PIRA have incorporated other illegal activity, beyond terrorism, into their operations on a large scale, with FARC heavily involved in drug and arms smuggling, while PIRA operates numerous front businesses in addition to narcotics and arms trafficking.[30] It is possible that FARC and PIRA have at least exchanged information on how to finance terrorist operations through illicit activities, if not shared smuggling routes or engaged directly in criminal deals. This shared criminal know-how and willingness to engage in illegality may also have played a role in the decision to engage in an exchange of technology and knowledge in their terrorist operations. Moreover, the revenue generated from their criminal enterprises could be used toward buying newer and, in some cases, more lethal weapons. In PIRA's case, the money brought in through front businesses and other illegal activities has eclipsed the revenue generated by the group's sympathizers in North America.[31]

---

[30] "Summary of Investigation of IRA Links to FARC Narco-Terrorists in Colombia" (2002).

[31] Personal interview with Northern Ireland security officials, Belfast, May 2005.

Rationalizing the Exchange of Technology and Knowledge

Both PIRA and FARC have their own reasons for wanting to obtain new technologies and learn from each other's battlefield experiences. According to one expert, the ability to construct an explosive device and deploy it against the intended target is at the heart of what constitutes success for a terrorist group.[32] These groups have been waging an insurgency against their respective states for 30 to 40 years and have outlived many other insurgent groups in that time, in part by continuing to improve on their technological and other operational capabilities.

PIRA Rationale

There are four key reasons that PIRA would be willing to share its technical experience with FARC. The first is that, until recently, the group wanted to remain technically and operationally relevant during the current cease-fire, which prevents PIRA from engaging in armed conflict. In September 2005, the Independent International Commission on Decommissioning determined that PIRA successfully decommissioned all its weapon stockpiles after years of stalled negotiations over whether or not PIRA would turn over its weapons to the government.[33] However, at the time that the Colombia Three were arrested in Bogotá, many observers believed that PIRA would never turn over its weapons because the group was committed to establishing a united Ireland and had said it would do so by force if necessary.[34] Because the group was committed at the time to a political rather than a military approach, it was limited in what it could do operationally to maintain its viability. During the period of active operations from 1969 to 1997, PIRA was able to innovate technologically because it was forced consistently to

---

[32] Personal interview with Northern Ireland security officials, Belfast, May 2005.

[33] Independent International Commission on Decommissioning, "Report of the Independent International Commission on Decommissioning," September 26, 2005.

[34] Personal interview with Northern Ireland security officials, Belfast, May 2005. It should be noted that, on July 28, 2005, PIRA pledged to decommission fully.

come up with new ways to confront the enemy and gain the operational advantage. Because it was no longer engaging the enemy, PIRA had to be creative about how it remained relevant. Prior to decommissioning in September 2005, the group wanted to be able to resurrect its operations as soon as it believed the cease-fire was no longer working.[35] To do this, PIRA needed to maintain the operational skills of its recruits and ensure that it had the appropriate technological capabilities to engage security forces when the time came. PIRA also wanted to maintain its credibility as a "revolutionary organization" with other like-minded groups and, by teaching these groups new skills, it helped to preserve its stature.[36]

The second reason that PIRA was apparently willing to share its expertise is related to the first reason, and that is that, unlike PIRA, FARC is still operationally active. FARC confronts its enemy on a regular basis and has the ability to test new weapons on its adversary and train its rank and file in new technologies and operational strategies. If PIRA helps in this regard and FARC then tests this knowledge and weapons in its operations, PIRA can see whether or not these tactics and weapons are successful. In this way, PIRA can continue to exercise its bomb-making and other terrorist skills and use FARC as its "testing ground" to practice these skills.

Similarly, PIRA may have shared this technology to gain some knowledge in return. In the case of FARC-PIRA exchange, PIRA provided FARC with technological know-how in exchange for a safe haven in which to test its own new weapons away from watchful British and Northern Ireland security officials and cease-fire observers. Although there is no information available in the public domain to confirm that PIRA was engaging in new weapon testing in Colombia, some security officials with whom we spoke suggested that PIRA may have been building and testing a new weapon there. These officials suggested that PIRA feared its weapon-testing activities may have been attracting the

---

[35] Ward and Hackett (2003).

[36] Ward and Hackett (2003).

attention of security officials at home and, as a result, sent the Colombia Three to the *despeje* to continue their efforts in a "safe" environment.[37]

A third reason may have been some sort of payment for services rendered. PIRA is now receiving less money from its supporters in the United States as a result of September 11, 2001, and may have seen the opportunity to advise FARC as a new source of funding. British intelligence has speculated that PIRA could have received as much as $2 million for its efforts, which would make up for some of the losses suffered as a result of reductions in funds collected from U.S. sources.[38] With all eyes on the Islamic terrorist threat, PIRA leaders may feel freer to conduct these kinds of activities because they believe the world's attention is focused elsewhere.[39] Moreover, the costs of running a nationwide organization such as Sinn Fein, which boasts 1,500 election workers, is expensive, and the group's criminal operations may not be enough to sustain it militarily and politically.[40]

FARC Rationale

FARC had one primary motivation for seeking PIRA assistance: It wanted to successfully implement urban terrorism against the Colombian government.[41] One can assume from its decision to look outside the organization that FARC had reached a stalemate with the Colombian government in its insurgent campaign, was not able to improve upon its existing capabilities from within, and wanted a shift in strategy to capture not only the government's attention but also gain some ground in its ongoing struggle. As a result, the group needed new weapons and technologies and turned for help to a group FARC leadership knew possessed these capabilities. According to one security offi-

---

[37] Personal interview with Northern Ireland security officials, Belfast, May 2005.

[38] "Staff Investigation: IRA in Colombia/The FARC Links," from Chairman Hyde to John Mackey, Investigative Counsel and Caleb McCarry, Subcommittee Staff Director, Senate Committee on International Relations Memorandum, April 15, 2002.

[39] "Staff Investigation" (2002).

[40] Martin Hodgson, Henry McDonald, and Peter Beaumont, "IRA Blunder in the Jungle Sparks US Rage," *The Observer*, August 19, 2001.

[41] Hodgson, McDonald, and Beaumont (2001).

cial, the "Provisionals" have an ability to overcome obstacles and adapt to change.[42] One can assume from examining the details of what we know about the FARC-PIRA case that FARC was interested in using more-sophisticated homemade mortars against its adversary, a tactic in which PIRA excelled. In fact, two of the Colombian Three were mortar experts.[43] Prior to 2001, FARC had only used primitive mortars in its operations—ones that were made out of canisters used for cooking gas. They were often inaccurate and had a "limited range."[44]

As mentioned previously, FARC killed more than 400 members of the Colombian security forces in an 18-month period, beginning in 2001. These attacks caused former Colombian president Andreas Pastrana in February 2002 to call off the government's three-year peace process with FARC.[45] In August 2002, in the face of an intense security effort, FARC attempted to assassinate Prime Minister Alvaro Uribe Velez at the presidential palace in Bogotá, just before he was sworn in, with a sophisticated remote-controlled mortar device, known as a barracks-buster—a weapon designed by PIRA. FARC had never used this type of device before, but it was standard in PIRA operations both in Northern Ireland and on the British mainland. One British bomb disposal officer who specialized in PIRA mortars said that it reminded him of the 1991 PIRA mortar attack on Downing Street.[46] According to one Colombian explosives expert, this attack, which killed 20 civilians and wounded 60, constituted a "technological leap" for FARC, and the same British bomb-disposal officer said the attack had the "fingerprints" of PIRA.[47] The attack also had a second element: two sets of mortar hits, the first aimed at distracting the security forces and the second aimed to hit the presidential palace. This "one-two punch" style

---

[42] Personal interview with Northern Ireland security officials, Belfast, May 2005.

[43] Martin McCauley was considered to be a mortar-bomb expert and James Monaghan was PIRA's head engineer and creator of the homemade mortar.

[44] Jeremy McDermott, "Colombian Attacks 'Have Hallmark of IRA,'" *BBC News*, August 11, 2002b.

[45] McDermott (2002b).

[46] McDermott (2002b).

[47] McDermott (2002b); Ward and Hackett (2003).

of attack has certainly been used by other terrorist groups, particularly Islamic militants, but is also a PIRA trademark and had not been part of FARC's training manual.[48] FARC's bombing of the Bogotá club El Nogal in February 2003 was also believed by many to bear the hallmarks of PIRA bomb-making expertise.[49] In May 2005, a former FARC rebel admitted to being trained by the Colombia Three in the use of explosives, landmines, and mortars.[50]

Identifying Exchanges in Colombia's *Despeje*

The circumstances surrounding the exchanges of knowledge and technology between PIRA and FARC are different from those in our other cases. Fundamentally, militant groups in Northern Ireland have been involved in peace talks with London since 1998 and the Good Friday Accords. Similarly, FARC and the Colombian government engaged in on-again-off-again cease-fires in the late 1990s. These exchanges took place, therefore, in the midst of a relative calm. Thus, it provides a vivid contrast to Hizballah and the al-Aqsa Intifada. Likewise, the geographic disparity between FARC-PIRA exchange on the one hand and regional militants colocated in the southern Philippines on the other hand is fairly significant. Having said that, both PIRA and FARC apparently benefited from this relationship. The following sections examine technologies and knowledge that PIRA shared with FARC, as well as how PIRA benefited from the interaction.

What PIRA Shared with FARC

Although PIRA has not admitted that it exchanged any knowledge or technology with FARC, it has been well documented over the years that PIRA is a technological innovator, particularly in the area of homemade explosives, and has successfully created and tested new

---

[48] McDermott (2002b); Jeff Johnson, "House Committee Investigates IRA, Colombia Terrorist Ties," *CNSNews.com*, April 24, 2002.

[49] Johnson (2002).

[50] Enda Leahy, "FARC Rebel 'Admits IRA Trained Him,'" *Times Online*, May 15, 2005.

weapons and strategies not only in its own theater of operations, but in others such as Libya. Many sources indicate that the Colombia Three passed on some of this technology and the skills needed to implement it to FARC.[51] For example, according to the U.S. Senate investigation, "Explosives management training for FARC by the IRA . . . has markedly improved FARC's proficiency in urban terrorism in the last few years."[52] The Senate investigation also found that IRA training apparently "result[ed] in more effective explosive attacks against the Colombian infrastructure including bridges, power lines, dams and other facilities as well."[53] Other sources report similar findings:

> U.S., British and Colombian investigators say the El Nogal bombing has the markings of I.R.A. and ETA tutelage. They point in particular to the sophisticated remote-controlled detonation of the car bomb.[54]

Another critical skill PIRA passed on to FARC was how to build a more effective mortar.[55] Specifically, FARC mortars now resemble

---

[51] McCauley and Connolly are reported to be two of PIRA's most experienced explosives experts, according to Mark Burgess, "Globalizing Terrorism: The FARC-IRA Connection," *CDI Terrorism Project*, June 5, 2002.

[52] "Staff Investigation" (2002).

[53] "Staff Investigation" (2002).

[54] Tim Padgett, "The Next Terror Nexus?" *Time Europe*, February 24, 2003.

[55] PIRA is one of the only militant groups to have achieved a high level of sophistication in homemade mortar development. PIRA engineers worked diligently over the course of their campaign to develop this technology; two of these mortar experts were in Colombia training FARC. PIRA used mortars primarily to attack security force installations and other hardened targets and was adept at using "throwaway" mortars, which were crude devices that had a devastating effect at a short range but were not difficult to assemble. These devices were typically mounted onto the back of a truck and armed with a timing device. During the 1980s, PIRA used the Mark-10 mortar with some success. The Mark-10 fired a six-inch shell with 24 pounds of explosives at a 300-meter range. This was the mortar that PIRA used in its attack on Downing Street in 1991. The Mark-18 mortar was an improvement on the Mark-10 mortar. Some sources also indicate that PIRA also recruited university-educated computer experts who could construct complicated timing devices for explosives and mortars and has used the cease-fire period to make technological improvements to these weapons.

PIRA's Mark-18 barracks buster,[56] designed to increase the group's effectiveness against security force bases. For example, FARC has allegedly added stabilizing fins to their mortars—a key feature of the Mark-18 mortar—to improve their accuracy.[57] According to a Colombian military colonel operating in a FARC stronghold, in 2002, there was "an unprecedented loss of three police bomb technicians and 19 police officers who were killed by FARC mortars in just the last 18 months alone." A Colombian police officer also reported that, in spring 2002, FARC mortars killed 119 peasant farmers at one time in an attack on a church, demonstrating a level of lethality in FARC attacks that the Colombian authorities had not previously seen.[58] As the investigation of the Colombia Three got under way, Colombian, British, and U.S. authorities began comparing PIRA technology with what they were seeing in recent FARC attacks. The U.S. investigation revealed that

> [t]he use of mobile mortars on trucks and pickups, which FARC is getting increasingly effective at using, is also strikingly similar to known IRA explosive techniques and practices, as is the targeting of police explosive experts. Neither we, nor the Colombians, can field credible explanations for this increased, more sophisticated capacity for these types of terror tactics by FARC, beyond IRA training.[59]

Colombian Police General Hector Castro opined that the August 2002 FARC mortar attack against the presidential palace was impossible to defend against at the time because "we didn't realize it was within the capacity of the Colombian terrorists to do it."[60] General Castro compared it with the September 11 attacks in that the United

---

[56] James Monaghan, one of the Colombia Three, was nicknamed "Mortar Monaghan" because of his skills in developing the Mark-18 mortar.

[57] Jeremy McDermott, "IRA Training and Tactics Help Colombian Rebels," *News.Telegraph*, May 10, 2005b.

[58] Padgett (2003).

[59] "Staff Investigation" (2002).

[60] McDermott (2002b).

States knew that type of an attack was possible but had no indication they were planning it.[61]

Another critical skill that PIRA was able to pass on to FARC was how to innovate under difficult circumstances. As referenced earlier, PIRA was able to hone its technical skills, particularly in the area of timed and automatic detonation of explosives in an urban environment, under the ever-watchful eyes of the British Army and the RUC.[62] Because FARC faced some of the same challenges in their cities, yet was probably not as adept as PIRA in addressing these challenges because of the group's reliance on its rural safe haven, PIRA may have been brought in to share not only its technical know-how but also skills in operational planning in an urban environment such as countersurveillance, target selection, ambush tactics, and intelligence gathering.[63] According to one security expert, finding the target is not as difficult as executing the attack and then leaving the scene.[64] PIRA operatives also have specialized technical knowledge that they could have passed on to FARC, such as what does and does not get destroyed (e.g., bleach and fire destroy everything) in the wake of a bomb attack, although there is no specific evidence in this case that this type of expertise was shared.[65]

Through this process of knowledge-building and technological advancement, by the end of its active campaign in the late 1990s, PIRA, according to one analyst, "had more than 30 varieties of weapons—including mortars and rockets—as well as numerous methods to lay and detonate explosives, advanced sniper tactics, etc., that it could draw on to mount operations."[66] Although the investigation into FARC-PIRA links and the expertise that FARC demonstrated as a result of

---

[61] McDermott (2002b).

[62] Jackson et al. (2005b, p. 100).

[63] Jackson et al. (2005b, pp. 111–112) and personal interviews with Northern Ireland security officials, Belfast, May 2005; see also Jeremy McDermott, "We Taught IRA How to Ambush," *The Scotsman*, April 25, 2002a.

[64] Personal interview with Northern Ireland security officials, Belfast, May 2005.

[65] Personal interview with Northern Ireland security officials, Belfast, May 2005.

[66] Jackson et al. (2005b, pp. 97–98).

this training provide some insight into what PIRA shared with FARC, PIRA could have shared any number of other technologies, training, and expertise because it was done in an ungoverned area where no record of the interaction between these groups was made, although there is no evidence this occurred. Some experts have referred to the *despeje* in Colombia as the new Afghanistan, where this type of learning can take place because it occurs in a safe haven.[67]

Adapting new technologies, particularly to an urban environment, was an integral part of why FARC agreed to host PIRA. However, FARC was also hoping to gain the ability to pass on this knowledge to other members, as PIRA had been able to do successfully in the course of its history. According to one expert, "even a simple weapon is complex without proper training."[68] PIRA builds up expertise through corporate memory and does not tend to lose this knowledge over time due to continued group cohesion and a low number of operatives with important technical knowledge who have been killed or captured.[69] It remains unclear whether FARC will have passed on to group members enough of what it learned to be able to sustain more sophisticated operations over time. But, PIRA was able to pass enough of this expertise on to FARC in the five weeks the Colombian Three spent in the *despeje* to result, at least in the short run, in more lethal and more effective operations against the Colombian military and urban, high-profile targets.[70]

What FARC Shared with PIRA

Although PIRA is one of the leaders in explosives innovation and has shared this expertise with others (e.g., FARC and ETA), it is not partic-

---

[67] "Summary of Investigation of IRA Links to FARC Narco-Terrorists in Colombia" (2002).

[68] J. Bowyer Bell, *The IRA: 1968–2000 Analysis of a Secret Army*, Portland, Oreg.: Frank Cass Publishers, 2000.

[69] Personal interview with Northern Ireland security officials, Belfast, May 2005.

[70] James Monaghan was appointed education officer on the IRA's Army Council and Brigade Staff in early 2001, according to "IRA Explosives Experts Arrested in Colombia," Institute for Counter-Terrorism, Herzliya, Israel, August 15, 2001.

ularly good at adapting or acquiring more advanced technologies, such as ground-to-air missiles to counter British helicopters.[71] Cease-fire conditions in Northern Ireland, moreover, compound PIRA's struggle to adopt these more advanced technologies. For example, PIRA allegedly tested a flame-weapon in Armagh in 2001. But the media attention this incident created apparently taught the group that it could no longer clandestinely test weapons in Northern Ireland.[72] Although it is uncertain exactly what kind of weaponry the Colombia Three were testing in the *despeje*, some reports allege that FARC tested fuel air explosives for both PIRA and ETA. Fuel air explosives are very lethal and described by some as the "poor man's atom bomb."[73] According to the 2002 U.S. Senate investigation into FARC-PIRA links, PIRA is "possibly using the [FARC] safe haven as a means to test and improve the IRA's own terrorist weapons and techniques in the rural jungles."[74] PIRA continues to prepare militarily for an armed struggle in the event that political negotiations fail to produce the desired results for the Republican movement. As such, the group is concerned about becoming "rusty" and, according to one official, is also recruiting new members from universities for their technological skills in the event they are needed in the future.[75] As one expert indicates, "Despite the cease-fire, the IRA remains anxious to find new weaponry technology."[76]

---

[71] For example, in the early days of the conflict, PIRA sought these and other advanced weapons in Libya and Palestine; it even established a research and development effort in the United States to develop these types of weapons. Authorities became aware of PIRA's desire, however, and made it increasingly difficult for PIRA to acquire new technologies.

[72] "IRA Explosives Experts Arrested in Colombia" (2001).

[73] Regan Morris and Liam Clarke, "Connolly's Wife in Cuba Says She Is Clueless Where He's Gone," *The Sunday Times*, January 30, 2005.

[74] "Staff Investigation" (2002).

[75] "Staff Investigation" (2002).

[76] Andrew Alderson, David Bamber, and Francis Elliott, "Terror International," *The Sunday Telegraph*, April 28, 2002.

Key Judgments

Many of the specific details of how technology was exchanged between FARC and PIRA are speculative, and, as a result, it is difficult to marry definitively the particulars of this case with the theory behind how groups exchange technology and knowledge. For example, we can speculate about why FARC or PIRA may have wanted to share information and technology, but it is difficult to know whether FARC contacted PIRA as soon as it learned that PIRA had developed the barracks-busting mortar in an attempt to gain this expertise; or, on the other hand, whether PIRA contacted FARC initially to offer its services in exchange for safe haven to test its own weapons and for financial gain.

Having said that, our research into technology exchanges between PIRA and FARC revealed some key findings. First, as with militant groups in Mindanao, *operational benefits* were weighed significantly by both groups in their decision to exchange technologies. For example, FARC clearly assessed, whether implicitly or explicitly, that the technologies PIRA offered to pass on had a significant comparative advantage over the technologies the group was already using, especially in its urban campaign. The barracks-busting mortar, in addition to the explosive devices PIRA had developed, were likely judged by FARC leadership to be an ideal fit for how the group planned to escalate its urban terror campaign.

As previously mentioned, FARC ultimately paid PIRA $2 million in exchange for its expertise. This price was not likely a significant barrier or risk for FARC leadership, because $2 million is a small amount of money for an organization that nets close to $170 million per year.[77] Similarly, it was not likely that its activities would be uncovered before the training was complete because it was being conducted in FARC-controlled areas. FARC probably had high confidence that, by the time the Colombian authorities discovered what it was doing, the group would have already conducted trial tests, taught others how to possibly

---

[77] Ted Galen Carpenter, *Drug Prohibition Is a Terrorist's Best Friend*, Washington, D.C.: CATO Institute, January 5, 2005.

build and use the technology, and even used the new weapons in actual attacks. PIRA had more to lose by risking that its activities would be discovered, which is precisely what happened, and that Sinn Fein would be penalized because PIRA violated its cease-fire agreement.[78] PIRA apparently assumed the risk because it had limited options for conducting tests at home.

Second, terrorist groups—like nonviolent organizations discussed in Chapter Two—want to codify know-how that relates to new technologies so that this knowledge can be shared within the group. In contrast to Palestinian militants, FARC leadership had a significant role in choosing what technologies to adopt as well as how to integrate them into FARC's institutional knowledge. This strategic oversight likely was responsible for FARC's success at codifying much of what PIRA taught them. FARC demonstrated this success through its increasingly sophisticated attacks, even after Colombian officials arrested the Colombia Three. Notably, Colombian officials state that PIRA also left behind some training manuals and other materials in the *despeje* that were passed on to FARC. These manuals allegedly included information on high-grade explosives and pipe bombs.[79]

Finally, the PIRA and FARC case also demonstrates that technology exchanges can increase terrorist groups' operational range and effectiveness significantly. This success was the result of trust built between PIRA and FARC. Some reports indicate that the Colombia Three, particularly James Monaghan, had reached out to FARC in the past and had been to Colombia several times, possibly to exchange other technologies and knowledge, although it is unclear precisely what kind of interaction took place. Through this series of interactions and the five weeks in the *despeje*, enough trust had been developed between these two organizations that FARC may have believed that PIRA wanted to help the group improve its capabilities and PIRA may

---

[78] Despite the fact that authorities discovered PIRA members in Colombia, Sinn Fein has not been penalized for violating the cease-fire.

[79] Henry McDonald, "IRA Manuals Discovered in Colombia," *The Observer*, December 16, 2001; Sean O'Driscoll, "Colombia Rebels 'Used IRA Manuals,'" *The Irish Examiner*, December 3, 2002.

have believed FARC wanted to help it remain operationally viable. The common ideological and religious roots that both groups shared also played a role in cementing the relationship between FARC and PIRA and the effectiveness of the exchange. Another factor that contributed to the success of this exchange was the nature of the technology itself. Although the technologies transferred between these groups were complicated, the concept of building homemade mortars and explosive devices was not new to FARC, simply an improvement over the group's current capabilities. Because FARC was building on existing knowledge, therefore, it increased the likelihood that it could absorb the new technology successfully. As in Mindanao, the existence of safe havens in Colombia contributed significantly to the success of technology exchanges between PIRA and FARC. This safe haven in the *despeje* allowed PIRA to transfer explosive-device technology to FARC via direct person-to-person contact. PIRA experts could, therefore, watch FARC members train and test these new technologies, recommending adjustments as necessary. The existence of a safe haven similarly provided PIRA and FARC with the opportunity to innovate further with fuel air explosives.

This case study on the exchange of technology and knowledge between FARC and PIRA did not follow along the lines that we originally expected. We had anticipated that it would be an example of a strictly financial transaction. Instead, we discovered that the rationale, types of technologies, and even transfer processes paralleled our other case studies closely, particularly Southeast Asia. This finding indicates that the patterns we identified through the course of our research might hold greater significance than we originally thought. The next chapter explores these overarching findings in greater detail and derives specific policy implications for U.S. homeland security.

CHAPTER SIX

Policy Implications

In February 2003, the U.S. government released its *National Strategy for Combating Terrorism*. In the section on "Operationalizing the Strategy," the national strategy argues that the ultimate objective of the global war on terrorism is to return terrorism to the "criminal domain." That is, the nature of terrorism should be altered in such a way that it is "unorganized, localized, non-sponsored, and rare."[1] The national strategy implies that linkages between terrorist groups cause them to shift from being unorganized and localized to being organized and regional or global. More importantly, these interactions provide terrorist groups with the opportunity to improve their overall capabilities far beyond the mere sum of each partner. Thus, terrorist groups that form partnerships and innovate far away from the United States still pose a potential threat to the U.S. homeland. This monograph attempts to explore this potentiality further in an effort to help the U.S. Department of Homeland Security prepare for and defend against emerging threats.

To do this, we focused on the methods that terrorist groups use to share technology and knowledge among themselves. Our research has policy implications in three main areas: (1) improving threat assessments, (2) disrupting innovation processes, and (3) affecting terrorist groups' cost-benefit analyses. The following sections outline these implications in greater detail.

---

[1] Executive Office of the President, *National Strategy for Combating Terrorism*, Washington, D.C.: Executive Office of the President, 2003, especially Figure 3.

Improving Threat Assessments

Our findings highlight the crucial importance of up-to-date and accurate threat assessments to guide U.S. homeland security countermeasures. For example, in the case of Hizballah and Palestinian militants, Israeli officials found themselves one step behind the terrorists, because they did not understand how these groups would respond to changes in the operational environment. Similarly, Colombian security officials were caught unawares because they did not understand how FARC might react to new technological opportunities and translate them in operations.

More than simply highlighting the importance of up-to-date threat assessments, however, our findings also have implications for how analysts can improve these assessments. First, a threat assessment that ignores intergroup dynamics—including technology exchanges and beyond—is destined to be outdated quickly. Indeed, focusing on these dynamics will likely be key for directing intelligence collection, aiding analysts, and informing policy accurately in the future. To capture these dynamics, threat assessments must examine the pressures on a group from counterterrorism operations and competition and explore possible strategies that the group may adopt as it reacts to those pressures, including strategies that seek new technologies and tactics from other groups.

Second, our research indicates that analysts should closely monitor the movement of individuals with technical expertise. Although we do not want to detract from the importance of monitoring individuals with technical skills in CBRN fields, we suggest that analysts also monitor individuals with technical expertise in remote-detonation technologies, rockets and missiles, camouflage for IEDs, and converted field ordnances (mortars). The militant groups in our study appeared most interested in improving these technologies.

Third, threat assessments should also anticipate the future operational needs of terrorist groups. To do this, we suggest examining failed attacks in addition to successful ones. If terrorist groups persist in a specific tactic, despite the failure, analysts are likely to see technological innovations to solve the problem. This pattern held true for

FARC in southwest Colombia, as well as for the Palestinians' use of rockets in WBGS. Beyond the failure of a particular tactic, it would be useful for analysts to track patterns of success or failure in different types of technology acquisitions. For example, it would be useful to know whether new technologies are more likely to be incorporated successfully if they come from an external source or whether they are generated internal to the terrorist organization.

Fourth, our research refined the understanding of exactly what constitutes "mutually beneficial" between terrorist groups. As we approached this study, we anticipated that terrorist groups would be most likely to exchange technologies when it was mutually beneficial. Yet we expected only the less-sophisticated group in the exchange to increase its operational capabilities. In comparison, we estimated that the more sophisticated group would receive monetary compensation or some other intangible benefit, such as helping a like-minded organization in its fight against a common enemy. But *operational benefit* was a key factor for even the most technologically sophisticated groups in two out of our three case studies. For example, JI provided Filipino militants with new technologies and knowledge. But it also benefited from access to safe havens. PIRA similarly provided FARC with advanced mortar technology and may have received operational benefit from FARC's fuel air explosive tests, if such these alleged tests occurred, also in safe havens.[2] This finding suggests that threat assessments focus on operational as well as strategic motivations for alliances between terrorist groups.

Disrupting Innovation Processes

This study also revealed a number of factors that facilitate technology exchanges. By targeting these factors or setting up barriers to them, the U.S. government will be more likely to disrupt innovation pro-

---

[2] Having said that operational benefit was a key factor for PIRA, one cannot underestimate the potential influence that an alleged payoff from FARC to PIRA might have had on their decisionmaking calculus as well.

cesses. For example, terrorists in our study mostly exchanged technology and knowledge using direct person-to-person contacts. In the case of Hizballah and Palestinian militants, Hizballah apparently only turned to physical technology exchanges and the exchange of information remotely once the risk of traveling to WBGS became too high. *Safe havens*[3] facilitated this direct person-to-person contact in our other two cases, thereby improving the likelihood that these groups would be able to innovate successfully. Importantly, in the case of Mindanao and southwest Colombia, central governments created these safe havens for militants in exchange for their participation in peace negotiations. The exploitation of these safe havens for technological innovation brings into question the wisdom of this policy, particularly if there is not consistent on-site monitoring by third parties.

Second, in all of our case studies, exchange processes included the movement of people and goods across borders. Table 6.1 compares modes of exchange across our three case studies. Given this requirement, border security policies should also help to disrupt potential technological innovations. The U.S. government might consider adding such aid to governments in areas where terrorist groups (1) are

Table 6.1
How Terrorists Exchange Technology and Knowledge

Exchange Method	Mindanao	West Bank and Gaza Strip	Colombia's *Despeje*
Remote or vicarious experience			
Exchange of descriptive information		X	X
Exchange of physical technologies		X	
Direct person-to-person contact	X	X	X

---

[3] Safe havens are a consistent theme in both the case of Southeast Asia and southwest Colombia. With regard to Israel, we did not emphasize the role of safe havens, although Hizballah maintains training camps in southern Lebanon and Palestinian militants have been known to train in these camps, because we focused on exchanges that took place within WBGS.

interested in attacking U.S. interests or (2) may explore technologies of particular concern.

Third, our study of Hizballah and Palestinian militants revealed that Israel's assassination of terrorist leaders, including strategic leaders as well as operational leaders with technical skills, disrupted Palestinian militants' ability to innovate. The U.S. government, therefore, could consider a policy that focuses on arresting militants with certain technical skills, in addition to those who provide links to al Qaeda. Currently, U.S. policy regarding the capture of terrorists appears to focus on individuals, such as Hambali with JI, who provide an organizational link between the al Qaeda hard core and affiliated groups. Our research indicates that, if the U.S. government wants to impede any ongoing innovation processes, it should also target individuals with technical (e.g., bomb-making) skills.

Affecting Terrorists' Cost-Benefit Analyses

The final policy implication of this study is that policies designed to break down trust between groups could negatively affect their decision to engage in technology exchanges. As we discussed in Chapter One, survival is a key objective for any terrorist group that faces a stronger state adversary. Policies aimed at increasing the risk of exchanges can take advantage of any given militant group's need to survive. The U.S. government should, therefore, consider developing policies that mitigate perceptions of a common enemy—as was a key contributor to trust between Hizballah and the Palestinians as well as among militants in Southeast Asia. Alternatively, policies could be developed that exploit natural points of potential religious, ideological, or ethnic discord. Such policies might not have affected the relationship between PIRA and FARC, but, in these situations, it might be possible to cause distrust by exposing vulnerabilities in the groups' information security. This approach could raise the perception of risk in the calculations of either militant organization.

Conclusion

In conclusion, this monograph both confirmed and challenged a number of different assumptions in our understanding of the wider terrorist threat. Our research indicates, for example, that terrorist groups are exchanging technology and know-how more successfully today than in the past. This pattern relates to al Qaeda–affiliated groups, such as JI and the Filipino terrorists, but also holds true for the non–al Qaeda– affiliated groups in our study. This particular finding is worrisome as it suggests that innovation is also occurring at a much more rapid pace, which could present a challenge to intelligence analysts in the U.S. government.

Similarly, experts often debate whether or not terrorist groups are likely to innovate in the face of counterterrorism pressure or on their own in a less intense environment. This debate underpins concerns over "failed or weak states" in the global war on terrorism, as well as stability operations and counterterrorism training programs by the U.S. government. In two of our case studies, terrorist groups innovated in response to intense counterterrorism measures—Southeast Asia and WBGS—but this pressure did not exist in southwest Colombia. This suggests that the answer to this debate is "both," although clearly room exists for more research to be done on the circumstances that provide the most conducive environment for innovation.

Finally, with regard to al Qaeda, some experts have argued that the global war on terrorism has prevented attacks inside the United States and, therefore, could be considered a success thus far. Although we do not necessarily disagree with this assessment, our research suggests that the global war on terrorism has more likely changed the nature of terrorism, not defeated it. In fact, the increased possibility for the exchange of technology and knowledge between groups, both because of and despite their ideological persuasion, makes the designation of terrorist groups as "local," "regional," or "global" less relevant. That is, these exchanges allow militant groups to expand their reach more rapidly than in the past, from local targets to global targets. Although the U.S. government has arguably reduced the overall capability of the al Qaeda hard core, the potential remains for other like-minded groups to increase their capabilities to the extent that they could threaten the U.S. homeland in the future.

Applying the Framework to Terrorist Groups

Figure 1.1 (Assessing Terrorist Threats Against the United States) in Chapter One of this book is drawn from a past RAND Project AIR FORCE study, *The Dynamic Terrorist Threat: An Assessment of Group Motivations and Capabilities in a Changing World.*[1] In that study, the authors evaluate 22 different terrorist groups, according to their degree of anti-U.S. sentiment and operational capabilities. Figure 1.1 represents the compilation of that study. Table A.1 provides a list of these 22 groups, along with their home base of operations.

Table A.1
Applying the Framework to 22 Terrorist Groups

Group	Home Base
al Qaeda	
Abu Sayyaf Group (ASG)	Philippines
Self-Defense Forces of Colombia (Autodefensas Unidas de Colombia) (AUC)	Colombia
Revolutionary People's Liberation Party/Front (DHKP/C)	Greece
National Liberation Army (Ejercito de Liberacion Nacional) (ELN)	Colombia
Basque Fatherland and Liberty (Euskadi Ta Askatasuna) (ETA)	Spain

---

[1]   Cragin and Daly (2004).

Table A.1—Continued

Group	Home Base
Revolutionary Armed Forces of Colombia (Fuerzas Armadas Revolucionarios de Colombia) (FARC)	Colombia
Armed Islamic Group (GIA)	Algeria
Salafist Group for Preaching and Combat (GSPC)	France
Islamic Resistance Movement (Hamas)	West Bank and Gaza Strip
Party of God (Hizballah)	Lebanon
Al-Gama'at al-Islamiyya (IG)	Egypt
Islamic Movement of Uzbekistan (IMU)	Uzbekistan
Kach	Israel
Lashkar-e-Toiba (LeT)	Kashmir
Liberation Tigers of Tamil Eelam (LTTE)	Sri Lanka
Communist Party of Nepal–Maoist (CPN-M)	Nepal
Moro Islamic Liberation Front (MILF)	Philippines
Revolutionary Organization November 17 (N17RO)	Greece
Palestinian Islamic Jihad (PIJ)	West Bank and Gaza Strip
Real Irish Republican Army (RIRA)	Northern Ireland
Shining Path [Sendero Luminoso] (SL)	Peru

Selected Bibliography

"4 More Suspects in V-Day Bombings Nabbed," *ABS-CBN News*, February 23, 2005.

Abu-Amr, Ziad, *Islamic Fundamentalism in the West Bank and Gaza*, Bloomington: Indiana University Press, 1994.

"Abu Sayyaf Guerrillas Training for Sea-Borne Terror Attacks," *The Khaleej Times*, March 17, 2005.

Abuza, Zachary, "The Moro Islamic Liberation Front at 20: State of the Revolution," paper prepared for the NIC-State/INR/EAT Conference on Mindanao, Washington, D.C., July 9, 2004a, pp. 3–5, 10–13.

———, "Al-Qaeda Comes to Southeast Asia," in Paul Smith, ed., *Terrorism and Violence in Southeast Asia: Transnational Challenges to States and Regional Stability*, London: M. E. Sharpe, 2004b, pp. 38–61.

"Al-Aqsa Unit Says Israeli Troops Held, Not Killed," Reuters, July 30, 2004.

Alderson, Andrew, David Bamber, and Francis Elliott, "Terror International," *The Sunday Telegraph*, April 28, 2002.

Almog, Doron, "Tunnel-Vision in Gaza," *The Middle East Quarterly*, Vol. 11, No. 3, Summer 2004. As of January 21, 2006:
http://www.meforum.org/article/630

Antiporda, Jeff, and Anthony Vargas, "Terrorist Trainer Nabbed," *The Manila Times*, March 23, 2005.

"Assessing Hizballah's West Bank Foothold," *PeaceWatch #463: Special Forum Report*, June 18, 2004. As of January 20, 2006:
http://www.washingtoninstitute.org/templateC05.php?CID=2154

Australian Government, "Australian National Security," undated Web page. As of January 22, 2007:
http://www.nationalsecurity.gov.au/agd/WWW/nationalsecurityHome.nsf

Aydogan, Neslihan, and Thomas P. Lyon, "Spatial Proximity and Complementarities in the Trading of Tacit Knowledge," *International Journal of Industrial Organization*, Vol. 22, Nos. 8–9, November 2004, pp. 1115–1135.

"Baalbek Seen as Staging Area for Terrorism," *The Washington Post*, January 9, 1984.

"Back to the Jungle," *The Economist*, March 1, 2003.

Baptista, Rui, "The Diffusion of Process Innovations: A Selective Review," *International Journal of the Economics of Business*, Vol. 6, No. 1, 1999, pp. 107–129.

Barak, Ehud, "What Security for the South? Syrian Displeasure Limits Army's Deployment," *The Lebanon Report*, Vol. 4, No. 9, September 1993, p. 5.

Bell, J. Bowyer, *The IRA: 1968–2000 Analysis of a Secret Army*, Portland, Oreg.: Frank Cass Publishers, 2000.

Ben-David, Alon, "Gaza: The Ghost of Lebanon," *Jane's Defence Weekly*, May 26, 2004.

Black, Ian, and Benny Morris, *Israel's Secret Wars*, New York: Grove Weidenfeld, 1991.

"Bombs in 3 Cities Kill 6," *The New York Times*, February 15, 2005.

Bulfinch, Thomas, *Mythology: The Age of Fable, the Age of Chivalry, Legends of Charlemagne*, New York: Crowell, 1970.

Burgess, Mark, "Globalizing Terrorism: The FARC-IRA Connection," *CDI Terrorism Project*, June 5, 2002. As of January 21, 2006: http://www.cdi.org/terrorism/farc-ira-pr.cfm

Cala, Andres, "Colombia's Cautious Revolutionary," *Consortiumnews.com*, July 25, 1999. As of January 21, 2006: http://www.consortiumnews.com/1999/072599a3.html

"Car Bombing Plot Foiled, Says AFP," *The Philippine Daily Inquirer*, March 30, 2005.

Carpenter, Ted Galen, *Drug Prohibition Is a Terrorist's Best Friend*, Washington, D.C.: CATO Institute, January 5, 2005. As of January 21, 2006: http://www.cato.org/dailys/01-05-05.html

Chalk, Peter, "The Davao Consensus: A Panacea for the Muslim Insurgency in Mindanao?" *Terrorism and Political Violence*, Vol. 9, No. 2, Summer 1997, pp. 80–82.

———, "Militant Islamic Extremism in Southeast Asia," in Paul Smith, ed., *Terrorism and Violence in Southeast Asia: Transnational Challenges to States and Regional Stability*, London: M. E. Sharpe, 2004, pp. 19–37.

Chandrasekaran, Rajiv, "Gunmen Take Foreigners Hostage in Malaysia," *The Washington Post*, April 25, 2000a.

———, "Military Finds Two Beheaded by Philippine Rebels," *The Washington Post*, May 7, 2000b.

———, "Philippine Troops Fire at Rebel Camp," *The Washington Post*, May 8, 2000c.

Chernick, Marc, "Appendix: Colombia's Major Guerrilla Movements," in Cynthia J. Arnson, ed., *Comparative Peace Processes in Latin America*, Washington, D.C.: Woodrow Wilson Center Press, 1999, p. 197.

"Clinton Kill Plot Claim," *The Courier-Mail* (Australia), May 22, 1996.

Cobban, Helena, *The Palestinian Liberation Organization: People, Power, and Politics*, Cambridge: Cambridge University Press, 1984.

Cragin, Kim, "Hizballah, the Party of God," in Brian A. Jackson, John C. Baker, Peter Chalk, Kim Cragin, John V. Parachini, and Horacio R. Trujillo, *Aptitude for Destruction*, Vol. 2: *Case Studies of Organizational Learning in Five Terrorist Groups*, Santa Monica, Calif.: RAND Corporation, MG-332-NIJ, 2005, pp. 37–55. As of January 22, 2007:
http://www.rand.org/pubs/monographs/MG332/

Cragin, Kim, and Sara A. Daly, *The Dynamic Terrorist Threat: An Assessment of Group Motivations and Capabilities in a Changing World*, Santa Monica, Calif.: RAND Corporation, MR-1782-AF, 2004. As of January 22, 2007:
http://www.rand.org/pubs/monograph_reports/MR1782/

Cummings, Jeffrey L., *Knowledge Transfer Across R&D Units: An Empirical Investigation of the Factors Affecting Successful Knowledge Transfer Across Intra- and Inter-Organizational Units*, unpublished doctoral dissertation, Washington, D.C.: School of Business and Public Management, George Washington University, 2002.

Davies, Roger, "Small Artillery Rockets Extend Range of Terrorist Attacks on Urban Centers," *Jane's Intelligence Review*, March 1, 2002.

Davis, Anthony, "Attention Shifts to Moro Islamic Liberation Front," *Jane's Intelligence Review*, April 2002, pp. 20–22.

———, "Philippine Army Prevents MILF Reorganisation," *Jane's Intelligence Review*, March 2003a, pp. 16–21.

———, "Resilient Abu Sayyaf Resists Military Pressure," *Jane's Intelligence Review*, September 1, 2003b, p. 17.

———, "Philippines Fears New Wave of Attacks by Abu Sayyaf Group," *Jane's Intelligence Review*, May 1, 2005, pp. 10–12.

de la Cruz, Aryln, "Janjalini Alive, Vows to Avenge Abu Jail Deaths," *The Philippine Daily Inquirer*, April 2, 2005.

"Disparate Pieces of Terrorism Puzzle Fit Together," *The Washington Post*, September 23, 2001.

"DND: Mindanao War Games to Target Jema'ah Agents," *ABS-CBN News*, June 28, 2004.

Edmonson, Amy C., Ann B. Winslow, Richard M. J. Bohmer, and Gary P. Pisano, "Learning How and Learning What: Effects of Tacit and Codified Knowledge on Performance Improvement Following Technology Adoption," *Decision Sciences*, Vol. 34, No. 2, 2003, pp. 197–223.

Elegant, Simon, "Asia's Own Osama," *Time Magazine*, April 1, 2002.

Evans, Richard, "Singapore Reports on Jemaah Islamiah," *Jane's Intelligence Review*, February 2003.

Executive Office of the President, *National Strategy for Combating Terrorism*, Washington, D.C.: Executive Office of the President, 2003. As of January 22, 2007:
http://purl.access.gpo.gov/GPO/LPS47951

"Fighting Rages in Jolo," *Filipinoexpress.com*, February 10, 2005. As of January 20, 2006:
http://www.filipinoexpress.com/19/07_news.html

Fisk, Robert, *Pity the Nation: Lebanon at War*, Oxford: Oxford University Press, 2001.

"Focus on Hizballah," *The Lebanon Report*, Vol. 4, No. 3, 1993, pp. 6–7.

Frontline, "Terrorist Attacks on Americans, 1979–1988: The Attacks, the Groups, and the U.S. Response," *Target America*, October 4, 2001. As of January 22, 2007:
http://www.pbs.org/wgbh/pages/frontline/shows/target/etc/cron.html

"Fuerzas Armadas Revolucionarias de Colombia (FARC)," *Jane's World Insurgency and Terrorism Database*, January 17, 2005.

George, T., *Revolt in Mindanao: The Rise of Islam in Philippine Politics*, Kuala Lumpur: Oxford University Press, 1980.

Gerges, Fawaz A., *The Far Enemy: Why Jihad Went Global*, Cambridge and New York: Cambridge University Press, 2005.

Gertler, Meric S., "Tacit Knowledge and the Economic Geography of Context or the Undefinable Tacitness of Being (There)," Nelson and Winter DRUID Summer Conference, Aalborg, Denmark, June 12–15, 2001.

Goldenberg, Suzanne, "Israeli Tank Blows up Leading Militant," *The Guardian Unlimited*, May 23, 2002. As of January 21, 2006:
http://www.guardian.co.uk/international/story/0,,720401,00.html

Gomez, Jim, "Suspect Says Terrorists Being Trained," *The Star-Bulletin* (Honolulu), March 24, 2005.

Good Friday Agreement, Northern Ireland Office, April 10, 1998. As of January 22, 2007:
http://www.nio.gov.uk/agreement.pdf

Government of the Republic of Indonesia, *Indictment of Abu Bakar Bashir*, Jakarta: Office of the Attorney General, April 2003.

Grant, Robert M., "Toward a Knowledge-Based Theory of the Firm," *Strategic Management Journal*, Vol. 17, 1996, pp. 109–122.

Griliches, A., "Hybrid Corn: An Exploration in the Economics of Technological Change," *Econometrica*, Vol. 48, 1957, pp. 501–522.

"Grumblings Surface During 'Baliktan,'" *The Philippine Daily Inquirer*, February 3, 2002.

"Hamas: Waiting for Secular Nationalism to Self-Destruct—An Interview with Mahmud Zahhar," *Journal of Palestine Studies*, Vol. 24, No. 3, Spring 1995, pp. 81–88.

Hamid, Ghazi, "Electronic Occupation," *Palestine Report*, June 22, 2005.

Hansen, Morten T., "The Search-Exchange Problem: The Role of Weak Ties in Sharing Knowledge Across Organizational Subunits," *Administrative Science Quarterly*, Vol. 44, No. 1, 1999, pp. 82–111.

Harel, Amos, "Hezbollah's Terror Factory in the PA," *Ha'aretz*, November 1, 2004.

Hedlund, Gunnar, "A Model of Knowledge Management and the N-Form Corporation," *Strategic Management Journal*, Vol. 15 (Special Issue), Strategy: Search for New Paradigms, 1994, pp. 73–90.

Herrera, Christine, "Misuari Failed to Deliver–OIC," *The Philippine Daily Inquirer*, January 2, 2002.

Hilder, P., "The Nail in the Wood: An Interview with Ismail Abu Shanab," *Open Democracy Ltd.*, 2004.

Hirshberg, Peter, "Getting Smart," *Jerusalem Post*, December 17, 1992.

"Hizballah Lends Its Services to the Palestinian Intifada," *Jane's Intelligence Review*, November 1, 2001.

"Hizballah Wages Electronic War in South Lebanon," *Jane's Intelligence Review*, February 1, 1995.

Hodgson, Martin, Henry McDonald, and Peter Beaumont, "IRA Blunder in the Jungle Sparks US Rage," *The Observer*, August 19, 2001. As of January 21, 2006:
http://observer.guardian.co.uk/nireland/story/0,11008,582089,00.html

Holden, Robert T., "The Contagiousness of Aircraft Hijacking," *The American Journal of Sociology*, Vol. 91, No. 4, January 1986, pp. 874–904.

"A Hostage Crisis Confronts Estrada," *The Economist*, May 6, 2000.

ICG—*see* International Crisis Group.

Independent International Commission on Decommissioning, "Report of the Independent International Commission on Decommissioning," September 26, 2005. As of January 21, 2006:
http://www.nio.gov.uk/iicd_report_26_sept_2005.pdf

Inkpen, Andrew C., "Learning, Knowledge Acquisition, and Strategic Alliances," *European Management Journal*, Vol. 16, No. 2, 1998, pp. 223–229.

Intelligence and Terrorism Information Center at the Center for Special Studies, "The 'Al Aqsa Martyrs Brigades' and the Fatah Organization Are One and the Same, and Yasser Arafat Is Their Leader and Commander," April 10, 2005. As of January 21, 2006:
http://haganah.org.il/hmedia/10apr05-mlm-fatah-a2.pdf

International Crisis Group, "Al-Qaeda in Southeast Asia: The Case of the 'Ngruki' Network in Indonesia," *Asia Briefing No. 20*, Jakarta/Brussels, August 8, 2002 (corrected on January 10, 2003). As of January 20, 2006:
http://www.crisisgroup.org/home/index.cfm?id=1765&l=1

———, "Jemaah Islamiyah in South East Asia: Damaged but Still Dangerous," *Asia Report No. 63*, Jakarta/Brussels, August 26, 2003. As of January 20, 2006:
http://www.crisisgroup.org/home/index.cfm?id=1452&l=1

———, "Southern Philippines Backgrounder: Terrorism and the Peace Process," *ICG Asia Report No. 80*, Singapore/Brussels, July 13, 2004, pp. 3–5. As of January 20, 2006:
http://www.crisisgroup.org/home/index.cfm?id=2863&l=1

International Institute for Strategic Studies, "Separatist Rebellion in the Southern Philippines," *Strategic Comments*, Vol. 6, No. 4, May 2000, p. 4.

"IRA Explosives Experts Arrested in Colombia," Institute for Counter-Terrorism, Herzliya, Israel, August 15, 2001. As of January 21, 2006:
http://www.ict.org.il/spotlight/det.cfm?id=656

"IRA Weapons Report Handed Over," *BBC News*, September 26, 2005.

"Iran and Hezbollah as Instigators of Terrorism," *Special Information Bulletin*, report by the Intelligence and Terrorism Information Center in Tel Aviv, January 12, 2005.

"ISA Arrests Head of Gaza Strip Hezbollah Cell," Israel Ministry of Foreign Affairs, March 10, 2004. As of February 14, 2005:
http://www.mfa.gov.il/MFA/Terrorism-+Obstacle+to+Peace/Terrorism+and+Islamic+Fundamentalism-/ISA+arrests+Gaza+Hezbollah+cell+10-Mar-2004.htm

Islam, Syed, "The Islamic Independence Movement in Pattani of Thailand and Mindanao of the Philippines," *Asian Survey*, Vol. 38, No. 5, 1998.

Jackson, Brian A., "Provisional Irish Republican Army," in Brian A. Jackson, John C. Baker, Peter Chalk, Kim Cragin, John V. Parachini, and Horace R. Trujillo, *Aptitude for Destruction*, Vol. 2: *Case Studies of Organizational Learning in Five Terrorist Groups*, Santa Monica, Calif.: RAND Corporation, MG-332-NIJ, 2005, pp. 93–140. As of January 22, 2007:
http://www.rand.org/pubs/monographs/MG332/

Jackson, Brian A., John C. Baker, Peter Chalk, Kim Cragin, John V. Parachini, and Horacio R. Trujillo, *Aptitude for Destruction*, Vol. 1: *Organizational Learning in Terrorist Groups and Its Implications for Combating Terrorism*, Santa Monica, Calif.: RAND Corporation, MG-331-NIJ, 2005a. As of January 22, 2007:
http://www.rand.org/pubs/monographs/MG331/

———, *Aptitude for Destruction*, Vol. 2: *Case Studies of Organizational Learning in Five Terrorist Groups*, Santa Monica, Calif.: RAND Corporation, MG-332-NIJ, 2005b. As of January 22, 2007:
http://www.rand.org/pubs/monographs/MG332/

"JI Linking with Other Terror Groups, Singapore Warns," *The Philippine Daily Inquirer*, March 30, 2005.

Johnson, Jeff, "House Committee Investigates IRA, Colombia Terrorist Ties," *CNSNews.com*, April 24, 2002. As of February 15, 2006:
http://www.cnsnews.com/Politics/Archive/200204/POL20020424c.html

"The Jolo Conundrum," *The Economist*, November 24, 2001.

Kane, Aimée, Linda Argote, and John M. Levine, "Knowledge Exchange Between Groups via Personnel Rotation: Effects of Social Identity and Knowledge Quality," *Organizational Behavior and Human Decision Processes*, Vol. 96, 2005, pp. 56–71.

Kogut, Bruce, and Udo Zander, "Knowledge of the Firm, Combinative Capabilities, and the Replication of Technology," *Organization Science*, Vol. 3, No. 3, 1992, pp. 383–397.

Lane, Peter J., and Michael Lubatkin, "Relative Absorptive Capacity and Interorganizational Learning," *Strategic Management Journal*, Vol. 19, No. 5, 1998, pp. 461–477.

Leahy, Enda, "FARC Rebel 'Admits IRA Trained Him,'" *Times Online*, May 15, 2005. As of January 21, 2006:
http://www.timesonline.co.uk/article/0,,2091-1612854,00.html

"Libya Denies Ransom Offer for Hostages," *The Sacramento Bee*, August 13, 2000.

Majul, C., *The Contemporary Muslim Movement in the Philippines*, Berkeley, Calif.: Mizan Press, 1985.

"Manila and Rebels Reach Agreement," *BBC News*, April 20, 2005.

Mansfield, E., "Technical Change and the Rate of Imitation," *Econometrica*, Vol. 29, No. 4, 1961, pp. 741–766.

Maqdsi, M., trans., "The Charter of the Islamic Resistance Movement (Hamas) of Palestine," *Journal of Palestine Studies*, Vol. 22, No. 4, Summer 1993, pp. 122–134.

Maskell, Peter, "Knowledge Creation and Diffusion in Geographic Clusters," *International Journal of Innovation Management*, Vol. 5, No. 2, 2001, pp. 213–237.

May, R. J. "The Wild West in the South: A Recent Political History," in Mark Turner, R. J. May, and L. R. Turner, eds., *Mindanao: Land of Unfulfilled Promise*, Quezon City: New Day Publishers, 1992.

McDermott, Jeremy, "We Taught IRA How to Ambush," *The Scotsman*, April 25, 2002a. As of January 21, 2006:
http://news.scotsman.com/topics.cfm?tid=150&id=425392002

———, "Colombian Attacks 'Have Hallmark of IRA,'" *BBC News*, August 11, 2002b. As of January 21, 2006:
http://news.bbc.co.uk/2/hi/americas/2186244.stm

———, "IRA Trio Leave Lethal Legacy in Colombia," *The Scotsman*, January 2, 2005a. As of January 21, 2006:
http://news.scotsman.com/topics.cfm?tid=667&id=3972005

———, "IRA Training and Tactics Help Colombian Rebels," *News.Telegraph*, May 10, 2005b. As of January 21, 2006:
http://www.news.telegraph.co.uk/news/main.jhtml?xml=/news/2005/05/10/wcol10.xml

McDonald, Henry, "IRA Manuals Discovered in Colombia," *The Observer*, December 16, 2001. As of January 20, 2006:
http://observer.guardian.co.uk/nireland/story/0,11008,619668,00.html

Memorial Institute for the Prevention of Terrorism, *MIPT Terrorism Knowledge Base*, undated. As of January 22, 2007:
http://www.tkb.org

"Mohajer (UAV)," *GlobalSecurity.org*, undated Web page. As of January 21, 2006:
http://www.globalsecurity.org/military/world/iran/mohajer.htm

Morris, Regan, and Liam Clarke, "Connolly's Wife in Cuba Says She Is Clueless Where He's Gone," *The Sunday Times*, January 30, 2005. As of January 21, 2006:
http://www.timesonline.co.uk/article/0,,2091-1463093,00.html

Murphy, John F., Jr., "The IRA and the FARC in Colombia," *International Journal of Intelligence and Counterintelligence*, Vol. 18, No. 1, Spring 2005, pp. 76–88.

"Muslim Militants Threaten Ramos Vision of Summit Glory," *The Australian*, January 13, 1996.

Mussomeli, Joseph, cited in Stephen Ulph, "Peace Talks Amid Renewed Violence in the Philippines," *Terrorism Focus*, Vol. 2, No. 8, April 28, 2005.

"No More Ransoms," *The Economist*, June 2, 2001.

O'Driscoll, Sean, "Colombia Rebels 'Used IRA Manuals,'" *The Irish Examiner*, December 3, 2002.

"Over 60 Hurt in Makati Explosion; GMA Inspects Site," *ABS-CBN News*, February 14, 2005.

Padgett, Tim, "The Next Terror Nexus?" *Time Europe*, February 24, 2003. As of January 21, 2006:
http://www.time.com/time/europe/magazine/article/0,13005,901030224-423493,00.html

"Palestinian Intifada[em dash]4th Anniversary," *Palestine Monitor*, undated. As of January 22, 2007:
http://www.palestinemonitor.org/new_web/4_years_intifada_anniversary.htm

"Palestinian Islamic Jihad," *Jane's Terrorism and Insurgency Centre*, undated.

Pazzibugan, Donna, "10 Sacks of Explosives Seized," *The Philippine Daily Inquirer*, March 24, 2005.

"Philippine Forces Hit Rebel Stronghold," *The Washington Post*, April 24, 2000.

"Philippine Government Calls Off Peace Moves," *Japan Today*, May 6, 2003.

"Philippines Seizes Rebel Headquarters," *The Washington Post*, July 10, 2000.

"Provisional IRA," *Jane's World Insurgency and Terrorism Database*, June 6, 2005.

"Qassam Rockets: Crude but Fearsome," *BBC News*, September 29, 2004. As of January 21, 2006:
http://news.bbc.co.uk/1/hi/world/middle_east/3702088.stm

Quismundo, Tarra, and Donna Pazzibugan, "Bomb Found Outside Makati Bldg.," *The Philippine Daily Inquirer*, March 28, 2005.

Rabasa, Angel, and Peter Chalk, *Colombian Labyrinth: The Synergy of Drugs and Insurgency and Its Implications for Regional Stability*, Santa Monica, Calif.: RAND Corporation, MR-1339-AF, 2001. As of January 22, 2007:
http://www.rand.org/pubs/monograph_reports/MR1339/

Radlauer, Don, "The 'al-Aqsa Intifada'[em dash]An Engineered Tragedy: Summary of Findings," May 21, 2003. As of January 22, 2007:
http://212.150.54.123/articles/articledet.cfm?articleid=440

Ranstorp, Magnus, *Hizb'allah in Lebanon: The Politics of the Western Hostage Crisis*, London: MacMillan Press, 1997.

———, "The Strategy and Tactics of Hizballah's Current 'Lebanonization Process,'" *Mediterranean Politics*, Vol. 3, No. 1, Summer 1998, p. 106.

Reagans, Ray, and Bill McEvily, "Network Structure and Knowledge Exchange: The Effects of Cohesion and Range," *Administrative Science Quarterly*, Vol. 48, No. 2, June 2003, pp. 240–267.

"Revolutionary Armed Forces of Colombia," Memorial Institute for the Prevention of Terrorism Terrorism Knowledge Base, undated(a).

"Revolutionary Armed Forces of Colombia," Wikipedia, undated(b). As of January 21, 2006:
http://en.wikipedia.org/wiki/FARC

Roberts, Joanne, "From Know-How to Show-How? Questioning the Role of Information and Communications Technologies in Knowledge Exchange," *Technology Analysis and Strategic Management*, Vol. 12, No. 4, 2000, pp. 429–443.

Rogers, Everett M., *Diffusion of Innovations*, New York: The Free Press, 1995.

———, "The Strategy and Tactics of Hizballah's Current 'Lebanonization Process,'" *Mediterranean Politics*, Vol. 3, No. 1, Summer 1998.

Saad-Ghorayeb, Amal, *Hizbu'llah: Politics and Religion*, London: Pluto Press, 2002.

Schwartz, Adam, *A Nation in Waiting: Indonesia in the 1990s*, Boulder, Colo.: Westview Press, 1994.

"The Secrets Behind Hezbollah's Recent Military Successes," *Middle East Intelligence Bulletin*, Vol. 2, No. 3, March 2000.

"The Seizing of the *Abu Hasan*," Israel Ministry of Foreign Affairs, May 22, 2003. As of February 15, 2006:
http://www.mfa.gov.il/MFA/MFAArchive/2000_2009/2003/5/The%20Seizing%20of%20the%20Abu%20Hasan%20-%20May%2022-%202003

"Seizing of the Palestinian Weapons Ship *Karine A*," Israel Ministry of Foreign Affairs, January 4, 2002. As of February 13, 2006:
http://www.mfa.gov.il/MFA/Government/Communiques/2002/Seizing%20of%2 0the%20Palestinian%20weapons%20ship%20Karine%20A%20-

Shatz, Adam, "In Search of Hezbollah-II," *The New York Review of Books*, Vol. 51, No. 8, May 13, 2004.

Simonin, Bernard, "Ambiguity and the Process of Knowledge Exchange in Strategic Alliances," *Strategic Management Journal*, Vol. 20, No. 7, 1999, pp. 595–623.

"Singapore Offers Grim View of Future Terror," *The Sydney Morning Herald* (Australia), January 11–12, 2003.

Spaeth, Anthony, "Rumbles in the Jungle," *Time Magazine*, March 4, 2002.

"Special Survey: Bombing of the AMIA Building in Buenos Aires," Israeli Ministry of Foreign Affairs, July 19, 1994. As of February 13, 2006:

http://www.mfa.gov.il/MFA/MFAArchive/1990_1999/1994/7/
SPECIAL%20SURVEY%20-%20BOMBING%20OF%20THE%20AMIA%20B
UILDING%20IN%20B

"Staff Investigation: IRA in Colombia/The FARC Links," from Chairman Hyde to John Mackey, Investigative Counsel and Caleb McCarry, Subcommittee Staff Director, Senate Committee on International Relations Memorandum, April 15, 2002. As of January 21, 2006:
http://www.ciponline.org/colombia/02041501.pdf

"Summary of Investigation of IRA Links to FARC Narco-Terrorists in Colombia," prepared by the Majority Staff of the House International Relations Committee, Committee on International Relations, U.S. House of Representatives, April 24, 2002. As of January 21, 2006:
http://www.ciponline.org/colombia/02042401.htm

"Summary of Report," *The Manila Times*, April 12, 2004. As of January 20, 2006:
http://www.westerndefense.org/articles/PhilippineRepublic/may04.htm

Susser, Leslie, "Hizballah Masters the TOW," *The Jerusalem Report*, March 13, 2000.

Szulanski, Gabriel, "Exploring Internal Stickiness: Impediments to the Transfer of Best Practice Within the Firm," *Strategic Management Journal*, Vol. 17 (Winter Special Issue), 1996, pp. 27–43.

Tan, S., *The Filipino Muslim Struggle 1900–1972*, Manila: Filipinas Foundation, 1977.

"Terrorists Train for Seaborne Attacks," Associated Press, March 18, 2005.

Turner, Mark, "Terrorism and Secession in the Southern Philippines: The Rise of the Abu Sayyaf," *Contemporary Southeast Asia*, Vol. 17, No. 1, June 1995, pp. 1–18.

———, "The Management of Violence in a Conflict Organization: The Case of the Abu Sayyaf," *Public Organization Review: A Global Journal*, Vol. 3, No. 4, December 2003, pp. 387–401.

"Two Israeli Arab Brothers Recruited by Hezbollah, Arrested," communicated by the Israeli Prime Minster's Media Adviser, March 5, 2004.

Ulph, Stephen, "Continuing JI Concerns in Singapore," *Terrorism Focus*, Vol. 2, No. 8, April 28, 2005a. As of January 20, 2006:
http://www.jamestown.org/publications_details.
php?volume_id=410&issue_id=3314&article_id=2369661

U.S. Department of State, *Country Reports on Terrorism*, Washington, D.C.: U.S. Department of State, Office of the Coordinator for Counterterrorism, April 27, 2005b. As of January 22, 2007:
http://purl.access.gpo.gov/GPO/LPS68317

U.S. Institute of Peace, "The Mindanao Peace Talks: Another Opportunity to Resolve the Moro Conflict in the Philippines," *USIP Special Report 131*, February 2005, pp. 5–7.

"Validation of the Existence of the ASG," internal document prepared for the Philippine National Intelligence Coordinating Agency (NICA), February 14, 1997.

Villareal, Bgen Ismael, "Conflict Resolution in Mindanao," *Forum 2*, Summer 1996, pp. 2–11.

Villaviray, Johnna, "When Christians Embrace Islam," *The Manila Times*, November 17, 2003. As of January 20, 2006:
http://www.manilatimes.net/others/special/2003/nov/17/20031117spel.html

von Hippel, Eric, *The Sources of Innovation*, New York: Oxford University Press, 1988.

"War Without End," *The Economist*, May 3, 2003.

Ward, Adam, and James Hackett, eds., "The IRA's Foreign Links: Externalising Its Expertise?" *IISS Strategic Comments*, Vol. 9, No. 5, July 2003.

Wege, Carl Anthony, "Hizbollah Organization," *Studies in Conflict and Terrorism*, Vol. 17, No. 2, 1994, pp. 151–164.

"When Local Anger Joins Global Hate," *The Economist*, October 19, 2002.

Ya'ari, Ehud, "Unit 1800," *The Jerusalem Report*, October 18, 2004.

"YM-III," *Jane's*, April 16, 2003.